Cy Warman

The white mail

Cy Warman

The white mail

ISBN/EAN: 9783743308978

Manufactured in Europe, USA, Canada, Australia, Japa

Cover: Foto ©ninafisch / pixelio.de

Manufactured and distributed by brebook publishing software (www.brebook.com)

Cy Warman

The white mail

The White Mail

BY

CY WARMAN

NEW YORK
CHARLES SCRIBNER'S SONS
1899

TO

BRYAN WARMAN

WITH A FATHER'S LOVE

CONTENTS

CHAPTER		PAGE
I.	THE PASSING OF THE WATCHMAN	1
II.	AGAIN THE REAPER	8
III.	SLEEPING OUT	13
IV.	THE FLOOD	21
V.	TOMMY'S REQUISITION	30
VI.	THEY HOIST THE FLAG	35
VII.	THE LABOR QUESTION	40
VIII.	LITTLE JACK'S PROMOTION	44
IX.	TOMMY FLAGS THE WHITE MAIL	49
X.	TOMMY MCGUIRE SEES THE CITY	55
XI.	THE HOLD-UP AT CASEY'S TANK	67
XII.	MCGUIRE GOES WEST	82
XIII.	MCGUIRE LEARNS TELEGRAPHY	90
XIV.	STATION-MASTER MCGUIRE	99
XV.	THE COMING OF THE SIOUX	108
XVI.	MCGUIRE GOES SWITCHING	119
XVII.	SNOWBOUND	132
XVIII.	BREAKING THE TRAIL	151
XIX.	A NEW LINE	157

CHAPTER	PAGE
XX. COMING HOME	161
XXI. ON A ROLLING SEA	171
XXII. THE NEW PRESIDENT	176
XXIII. THE MAID OF ERIN	184
XXIV. OVER THE BIG BRIDGE	194

The White Mail

CHAPTER I

THE PASSING OF THE WATCHMAN

DENIS McGUIRE lived at Lick Skillet, on the ridge between the east and west forks of Silver Creek, midway between Troy and St. Jacobs, twenty-two miles east of St. Louis — Vandalia line. Denis McGuire was the section boss, Tommy McGuire was his only heir, Mrs. McGuire, in addition to being Tommy's mother, made herself generally useful about the house.

Lick Skillet possessed a saw-mill and a blacksmith shop, and contained, if we count the "nigger" who drove Jim Anderson's bull team at the mill, twenty-seven souls.

Denis McGuire was an honest Irishman, industrious and sober, except on Saturday nights, and possibly Sunday. He was unable to read or write, even his own name. Heidelberg, the station agent at St. Jacobs, the eastern terminus of McGuire's section, kept his books and accounts and the time of the men. In return for this kindness McGuire used to do odd spurts of manual toil for Heidelberg. Sometimes, on a Saturday afternoon, he would set his car off at the end of his run, take his men over (between trains) and shovel snow and saw wood for the agent. In summer, when they had their scythes out, they invariably cut the weeds on the vacant lot between the station and Heidelberg's house, clipped the lawn, and weeded the garden.

Down by West Silver Creek bridge there was a water tank and a pump, whose motive power was a mule. Close by the bank of the lazy little river stood the watchman's shanty, narrow, high, and painted red, like the tank, and like hundreds of other shanties that were strung along the line from St. Louis to Indianapolis. Rain or shine old man Connor was always there to show his white light to the engineer of the Midnight Express, and a white flag to the men on the White Mail in the morning. Beyond the bridge, a round-faced lad of sixteen summers trudged after the mule, who appeared always to be going sidewise, as a boar goes to battle. The round-faced boy was the old watchman's eldest son, a good-natured, lazy lad who could not whistle a tune, but who was forever singing, "The Hat Me Father Wore."

When the old man had walked across the bridge and back, with his hands behind him, glanced at the block on the figure-board to see that the tank was full of water, filled his red light and his white light, polished the globes, and set them both burning by the door, he would light his pipe and sit and gaze down into the dirty delinquent river, that came cautiously under the bridge, crept noiselessly away and lost itself in the mournful, malarial forest.

Patient as a monk, solitary as a bandit, lonely as an outcast, the faithful watchman dwelt by the bridge. To the gray-haired driver of the Midnight Express, whose black steed lifted him in a short half hour out of the great American bottoms, by the coal mines at Collinsville and up to the tablelands of Troy, who strained his eye around the curve at Hagler's Tank, he showed the friendly white light. "Let her go," it seemed to say, and the great headlight, trembling down the long grade, flashed a moment on the storm-stained face of the old watchman, and was gone again. Nor did he sleep or nod or close his eyes until the dawn of day; until he had shown the milk-white flag to the men on the White Mail in the morning.

But time will tell upon us all. It told upon the bridge, upon the old man and the mule. In spring the carpenters would come and fix and brace the bridge, that had been racked and strained by ice and flood. In spring the local doctor gave the old man something for his cough, and the old man cut a quaking asp and fixed it in the stall for the mule to gnaw; for its bark was the bitters the mule needed in spring.

At the far end of a raw, cold March the old man fell sick of a fever; typhoid-pneumonia the doctor called it, a cruel combination, either half of which could kill.

It was midsummer before he was able to take his post at the bridge again.

In the autumn he had ague that shook his bent frame and made his old bones ache. All night he would watch in the little shanty, all the morning shake with ague, and burn with fever in the afternoon.

When winter came the ague went away, but it left the old man bent and pale. His cough grew worse, and finally a severe cold put him on his back with pneumonia.

When the day set down by the doctor for a change, "one way or the other," had arrived, the medical expert lost nothing by the prediction. Like the Oracle at Delphi that assured the king that his war would wreck an empire, without saying which empire, the doctor's reputation was reasonably safe. As the day wore away the old man grew restless. At night the fever came on. At midnight he leaped from his bed, seized the lamp that stood upon the little table near him, and rushed out into the rain-swept night to show it to the driver of the Midnight Express. When the train had crashed over the cattle-guards at the road crossing, the watchman went back into the house, but refused to go to bed again. "I can't go yet," he said, "I must wait for the White Mail."

They sent for the doctor, and the doctor told them to send for the priest.

When the dawn came the old man opened his eyes.

"Me flag," he cried, "where is me flag?" and Mrs. Connor brought a clean white flag and placed it in his hand.

Now the White Mail that had come out of the east in the afternoon, crossed Indiana in the evening, and entered Illinois in the night, dropped from the great prairie into the sag at East Creek, lifted again, screamed across the ridge, and plunged down the long hill towards West Creek bridge.

The old watchman, hearing the roar and the whistle, grasped his flag and darted from the door. As he reached the open air the White Mail went roaring past. A white ribbon of steam fluttered from the engine dome and floated far back along the top of the train. The old man flourished his flag, staggered, swayed, fell into the arms of his wife, and they carried him into the house again.

When the priest came the old watchman was sleeping with his cold hands crossed above his breast and candles burning about his bed.

CHAPTER II

AGAIN THE REAPER

AT the suggestion of the section boss, the agent asked the roadmaster to put Jimmie Connor on the bridge as watchman, and give little Jack, his brother, the mule and the tank.

After that, instead of the bent form of the old man, the widow saw her boy coming up from the bridge of a morning when the White Mail had gone by.

Everyone was kind to the boys and gave them encouragement.

Conductor Wise, who went up on the Midnight Express and came down on the White Mail, sent a dog to be company for the young watchman. Charley Cope, who fired the Highland Accommodation, gave little Jack a long whip, and the foreman of the bridge gang built a platform so that he could stand, or sit in the centre of the "horse power" like the driver of a threshing machine.

But with all this kindness, the greatest measure of help and comfort, encouragement and amusement, came from little Tommy McGuire. Round-faced, freckled, happy, careless, "onry," the neighbors called him. He found some paint one day that the painters had left when they painted the section house, painted the white calf red and striped the goat like the zebra, whose life-sized likeness adorned the blacksmith shop.

The agent, who was something of a philosopher, always argued that Tommy McGuire was not as bad as he was painted. He was not wicked, but curious, Heidelberg said. When he put precisely the same sized can to Jimmie Connor's dog that he put to his own dog, it was not to punish the brutes, but merely to see which would get home first, and settle a dispute of long standing.

When he took his red spaniel under his naked arm and dived from the top of the bridge when the river was running bank full, it was merely to see which could stay under water longest, himself or the dog. And so, behind all of his mischief, the agent was able to see a motive. It was the boy's unquenchable thirst for knowledge that made him want to explore everything, from the cave in the bluff to the crow's nest in the top of the tallest sycamore.

It may be that the Connor boys were no better because of his visits, but they were happier; he was company for them and made them forget. He awed them with his wonderful feats of climbing, diving, swimming, and jumping. When Jimmie, the watchman, would shrink back and hold his cap as the cars roared past, Tommy McGuire would stand close to the rail and laugh in the face of the screaming steed. Once, just to see how it would feel, he hung from the bridge by his legs while the Midnight Express went by.

One morning Mrs. Connor saw Jimmie swinging down from the cab of a freight engine. His feet slipped from the iron step, he fell, and his mother put her hands over her eyes and screamed. In a moment he was on his feet again, waving his cap encouragingly to his mother and signalling to the engine crew to go ahead. But he was not unhurt. When they removed his trousers they found that the flange of a tank wheel had sliced the whole calf off one of his legs right down to the bone.

While the rest were busy with the wounded boy, Tommy McGuire went down to the tank to break the news to little Jack. "Don't you be afraid," said he to the pale boy who was two years his senior, "if anything happens to Jimmie I'll take care uv you. Dad says I'm no good, mother says I'm sassy, Mis' Dutton says I'm 'onry' and the priest says I'm 'incourageable,' and I guess the're all about right, but you know me, Jack, eh? old man! an' you know I'll do what I say."

There were tears in the eyes of the pump boy when Tommy took his two hands, gave him a jerk forward, let him go and hit him a hard jab in the ribs, and then, as he turned, gave him a kick that looked worse than it was.

"An' I've got a frien' Jack me boy, 'at can git us anythin' from a push car to a private train — that's Mr. Heidelberg — he's me frien'."

Ten days from the day the accident occurred, they cut Jimmie's leg off, but it was too late. He never revived, and before the bewildered children and the grief-sick mother could realize what had happened, they had crossed his helpless hands over his youthful breast and lighted the candles.

That night McGuire and his men came and "waked" Jimmie, as they had waked his father only a few short months before.

U. P. Burns came with his black pipe and his black bottle and smoked and drank and sang "come-all-ye" songs.

CHAPTER III

SLEEPING OUT

THE world looked dark to the widow Connor when her husband and her eldest son were sleeping among the crosses in the little Catholic graveyard.

Mrs. McGuire sent Denis to see Heidelberg, and when the roadmaster came up from East St. Louis these three officials held an important and animated meeting.

This conference was interrupted by Tommy McGuire, who burst in upon them like a sunrise in the desert.

"I got a scheme," said he to the agent, who, having grown up under a cloud similar to that which hung over the freckled youth in front of him, beamed upon the boy encouragingly and bade him reveal his plans. "Yo' see," said Tommy, ignoring the roadmaster (he never noticed his father, probably because his father never noticed him), "Jack can't keep th' pump, 'cause he can't harness d' mule, an' he can't mind d' bridge 'cause it 's too lonesome. Now I aint got nofin t' do, an' I can run d' pump in daytime, an' Jack can sleep n 'en I can sleep in d' shanty nights, an' Jack can wake me when d' Midnight Express goes by, n 'ne I can go t' sleep agin."

Tommy had talked very rapidly, and now as he paused for breath he glanced at the road-master.

"And who's goin' t' 'arness th' mule fur ye, me lad?" asked the gruff official.

Tommy gave him a dark look and turned to the agent, as much as to say, "This is our end of the road."

"I seen Mr. Collins," he said to the station-master, "an' he's goin' t' build me a platform long side d' stall so I can harness d' mule and jump on his back an' go to me work 'thout asken any odds uv U. P. er anybody, an' till he gets d' platform done d' mule can sleep in his harness a few nights — taint no worse fur 'im than fur me t' sleep in me clothes, an' that 's what I 'm goin' to do."

"Very well, Tommy," said the agent, "you wait outside and we will see what can be done."

"Well," began the roadmaster, when the august body had reconvened, "if ye's fellies wants to open a kindergarden, ye kin do it, but mind, I tell ye, it's agin me judgment t' put a lad like little Jack Connor watchin' a bridge o' nights."

"I'll be responsible fur Jack," said McGuire, speaking for the first time; "th' lad have the head uv a man above his slender shoulders, an' Pat Connor's boy can be trusted, do ye mind that?"

"And I'll be responsible for Tommy McGuire," said the agent, looking at the father of the freckled youth.

"He's a tough kid that," said the roadmaster, "wud all jew respect to his mother."

"Leave him to me," said the station-master, "he's no whit tougher than I was at his age."

When Tincher, the agent's under-study, went out to look for Tommy, to apprise him of what he had overheard, the boy was not to be seen. Of course he could not be expected to sit quietly in the sun for nearly an hour, and he had not. He had climbed to the top of the grain elevator, he had mixed salt with U. P. Burns's tobacco, and pinned a "lost" notice to his father's coat that hung on the handle-bar of the hand car. Then he had scattered shelled corn for the miller's pigs. He had discovered the agent's marking pot, and was now lying flat on his stomach, reaching over the edge of the platform, making zebras of all the white pigs in the drove.

The widow laughed and cried when Tommy told her how it had all been arranged, and Tommy's mother, to his surprise, actually kissed him. Even Denis McGuire was able to feel a pardonable pride in the boy. Mrs. Dutton said she was glad to "see th' brat thryen to make suthen uv hissilf." The priest promised to pray for him. "I'll stand good for him here, father," the agent had said to the priest, "if you'll stand good hereafter," and the priest had promised.

The first day was all too short for Tommy, though sad enough for Jack. By three o'clock in the afternoon the tank was full and the mule turned out to graze.

Mr. Collins, the foreman of the bridge carpenters, had built a bunk in the little shanty, and Mrs. McGuire and the widow had come down to fix the bed for Tommy. The enthusiastic boy gave Jack little time to hug his grief, but kept talking of the future, of their importance to the company and to Jack's family. His plans were not quite perfect in his own mind, but he felt that in some way he must contribute to the support of the widow's family. He had no need of money for himself. He had never had any or cared to have, unless it would be to buy a target rifle like Anderson's boy had, or maybe some firecrackers for the Fourth, and for Christmas. But poor little Jack would not enthuse. As often as Tommy looked up he found his companion staring at him as if half afraid.

"Whatcher skeered about, Jack Connor?" demanded Tommy, boxing the boy's cap off.

"When ye goin' to bed?" asked Jack, his wild eyes growing wider as he pictured to himself the loneliness of the place when Tommy should go to sleep.

"Aw, shucks," said Tommy, "I'm not goin'

t' bed at all; come outside an' le's build a bonfire to keep th' skeeters off."

They made such a fire of dry brush and driftwood that when the Midnight Express came round the curve at Hagler's tank the engineer thought the bridge was burning, and shut off. But a moment later little Jack was at the end of the bridge moving the white light up and down, as he had seen his father do, and the driver opened the throttle again. Despite the fact that Tommy was close behind him, the timid boy began to tremble and draw back as the headlight glared in his face. Tommy seized the signal lamp and stood smiling in the face of the driver as the great engine struck the bridge and roared past, shaking the earth for rods around. Away the wild steed went, out toward the morning. She had started fresh and clean from the Mississippi, she would slake, for a brief moment, her burning thirst at the Ambraw, and at dawn drink of the waters of the Wabash.

When the red lights on the rear of the flying train had drawn close together and finally dropped over the bridge, Tommy turned to find little Jack crouching at the door of the shanty.

" 'Smatter uv you, Jack Connor?" demanded the freckled boy. "Guess I better tie you under th' bridge till yo' git ust to the cars."

They put the white light down on the floor, and began to practise their writing lesson; learning to write their names so they could sign the pay rolls when the car came up the road again. Tommy started to sing, "The Hat Me Father Wore," but remembering suddenly that this was the only song Jimmie Connor had ever tried to sing, he changed off to "Jerry Ile the Kayre," —

> " Wid a big soljer coat
> Buttoned up to me troat,
>   All danger I would dare ;"
> Thin jint ahead an' cinter back;
> Oh! Jerry go ile th' Kayre."

But try as he would Tommy could not keep the clouds away from the face of his friend. The poor lad seemed half dazed by the dreadful scenes through which he had passed. It was nearly morning. The bonfire had burned down to gray ashes, and the boys were sleepy.

Tommy took the red light, shook it, and

turned it up. A lost dog over by the saw-mill set up that awful unearthly howl that boys are wont to connect in some way with abandoned farms and funerals. A hoot-owl hooted on the top of the tank, and little Jack began to cry.

CHAPTER IV

THE FLOOD

WHEN the White Mail came out of the east, carrying signals for the sun on the following morning, the driver looked down on a pair of very dirty faces at the end of West Creek bridge. The white flag fluttered in the morning breeze, and little Jack's arm shook like an aspen branch as the big engine struck the bridge and thundered by. Tommy, who feared nothing, day or night, stood near him, pushing him encouragingly as he shrank from the flying train. When they had walked across the bridge and back, to see that no sparks had fallen from the quivering ash-pan, they returned to the pump. The old mule had been harnessed before it was light, from the new platform that Tommy had designed and the boss carpenter had built. He had stopped short and fallen dead asleep the moment the boys left him to flag the fast mail. He was now rudely awakened by Tommy, who hit him a sharp cut with the long whip, as he climbed to his place on the platform.

In a little while the sun came up over the tree-tops and touched the water tank. Little Mary Connor came down the track, bringing breakfast for the boys, and they were glad to see her. When she had fixed the plates and poured the hot, black coffee into the bright tin cups, she allowed Tommy to lift her onto the platform, where she encouraged the mule while the boys had breakfast.

"Say, Jack, old man; this is great," said Tommy, taking a long pull at the bracing beverage. Jack gave his companion a furtive glance, but deigned no reply — not even a smile. "Jimminy-crismus, why don' yo' eat?" shouted Tommy. Jack was staring at his sister, who looked so weird and ghost-like in her black frock, with eyes that seemed too large for her, and her white face hiding in a heap of hair.

The boys were much refreshed by the hot breakfast, and when Tommy helped little Mary from the platform he was in a humor to tease her. He even went so far as to pull her ear gently and to pinch her cheeks, — to put life in 'em, as he expressed it. Mary smiled and colored slightly: the first faint flush of little girlhood. She liked Tommy, and he liked her. Rough and boisterous with boys, he was always gentle and thoughtful with the little girls, and Mary, to his mind, was the belle of Lick Skillet.

When Tommy had helped Mary over the bridge, dropped the spaniel into the water for his morning bath, and shied a few stones at the kingfisher on the top of a telegraph pole, he pushed Jack from the platform, ordered him to bed, and began to tickle the mule with the long lash. Little Jack declared that he was not sleepy. "I'm boss o' th' day shif', Mr. Jack," said Tommy, "an' my talk goes, — you're th' night hawk, — sabe?"

Jack went reluctantly to the bed that had been fixed for the other boy, but had not been used, and Tommy continued to larrup the mule and watch the marker crawl down the figure-board as the water crept toward the top of the tank. At the end of an hour little Jack came from the shanty, declaring that he was not sleepy.

"Well," says Tommy, "if yo' won't sleep, yo'

kin work," and he gave Jack the whip. "This ole giraft aint had no breakfast, an' I guess he'll want some time th' tank's full."

A half hour later Tommy returned with a big feed of oats in a bag. When he reached the west end of the bridge he stopped, put down the bag, and made the woods ring with his boyish laughter.

The old mule was lying peacefully in the endless path, while little Jack, curled up like a bird dog on the platform, was sound asleep.

Tommy took off his coat, fixed it under Jack's head for a pillow, and then cautiously wakened the mule. He dared not use the lash now, but, following close behind the mule, prodded him persistently with the whip-handle. Round and round they went, the marker crawled down, the water up, and little Jack snored like a saw-mill.

By twelve o'clock the big tank was full of water, and the old mule was having his breakfast and dinner all at one feed.

"I give yo' fair warnin', Mr. Jack Connor," said Tommy, swimming on his back, "if yo' don' skin off yer duds an' git in here I 'll come up there an' trow yo' off d' bridge, duds an' all."

"I don' feel like ut, Tommy," said Jack, "t' mar' I 'll go in, maby."

Tommy and the dog took a few dives from the bridge, when Jack, who had been standing guard, shouted to his companion to "hustle on his duds" for Mary was coming down the track with the dinner.

Tommy, properly attired, was waiting at the narrow foot-bridge that lay across the ditch from the grade to the little shanty. He took the basket and the jug of buttermilk, and Mary, young as she was, felt and appreciated these little attentions from the young gallant. She spread a newspaper on the little pine table and put down the plates.

"Watcher doin' uv three plates, Mary?" asked Jack.

"Mamma said I could hev dinner wif you'uns," said Mary, shyly.

"'S matter uv yo', Jack Connor? Think girls never gits hungry?" demanded Tommy, tumbling over his companion and rolling him in the high grass.

There was no fried chicken, no green peas, no radishes, nor corn, nor bread and butter; there was nothing — not even chicken bones — when the banquet was over, for the dog had eaten the bones.

Mary picked up the dishes and the empty jug, and when Tommy had climbed up in the old sugar tree to see if the young birds were out, she swept the little shanty and gathered a bouquet of wild flowers and placed them in a tomato can on the little table.

When Tommy had helped her over the bridge the boys put the mule out to grass. They tied his long reata to the rope that hung from the water tank — the rope the fireman pulls when the engine stops for water — and then sat under the tank, playing mumblety-peg, while the mule regaled himself on the luxurious grass. Jack soon grew tired of the sport, put his head on the oat-bag and fell asleep. In a little while Tommy followed him, for they were exceedingly comfortable and content with the big tank full of water and their own little tanks full of wholesome food and buttermilk. They had scarcely begun to dream, however, when an extra west came creeping up over the ridge. The engineer was fanning them down the long slope in order to be able to lift them over the hill at Hagler's tank, when he observed the old pump mule slowly crossing the track beyond the bridge. He sounded the whistle and the mule stopped, with his hind legs not far from the outer rail. The whistle screamed frantically, and the brakeman climbed out of the caboose to the top of the cars to be near the brakes in case of danger. The boys slept peacefully under the tank. The mule raised his head and looked at the locomotive. He had a placid contempt for screaming locomotives, whose very breath of life was drawn from tanks which he, and his kind, were forced to fill. The travel-worn engine had ceased its screaming and was now driving madly, and with malice aforethought, toward the mule. At the last moment — not from fear of the machine, but because he hated it — the mule moved a space away. This move on the part of the mule tightened the rope slightly, so that the pilot of the engine picked it up and stretched it across the front end of the flying locomotive. A moment later the mule, at one end of the rope, received a jerk that turned him over, and the tank valve, at the other end of the rope, was pulled wide open. A great stream of water, as big around as one of the boys, now shot down against the side of the passing train, and, rebounding, spread out under the tank. The boys, thus suddenly awakened by the cold flood, which, before they could get to their feet, began to roll them over and almost smothered them, thought they must be in the midst of a cloud-burst. The roar of the train was so deafening they could not call to each other. If they stood up, the weight of the falling water knocked them down again. When the train had gone by the noise grew less terrific and Tommy fought his way to the open air. A glance at the surroundings showed him what had happened, and he hastily dragged little Jack, drenched, half drowned, and thoroughly frightened, from under the tank. One end of the broken rope had wrapped around the water-spout and held the valve open. Tommy climbed upon the tank-ladder, extricated the rope, and that closed the valve.

The old mule, which had caused all the trouble, was hitched up again and started 'round on his endless journey to put up the few hundreds of barrels of water that had been wasted.

Tommy and Jack stretched themselves on the platform to encourage the mule and dry their clothes.

CHAPTER V

TOMMY'S REQUISITION

"Ahn a winter's mornin' whin the wind was blowin'
  At a staid an' stiddy gai-at,
Did a Kayre sit sail wud a kayrgo laden
  Out of siction siventy-eight."

U. P. BURNS stopped on the bridge and cocked his ear. He knew the song and the singer. It was U. P.'s day to walk the track, and he was now inspecting the bridge in an officious manner, not altogether pleasing to the young gentlemen who held themselves responsible for that structure — day and night.

"Hay, there! ol' flatobacker!" cried Tommy McGuire, from the top of a waving elm, "d' yo' know the trains are all over-due this morning?"

"I know they're all on time."

"I say they're all over-due," insisted the pump boy.

"Well, what make ye tink so, Tommy?"

"'Cause they bin out all night — ha, ha, ha

—yo'le bum; that's th' time yo' tuck th' pin hook." And Tommy climbed still higher to be out of reach of the rocks and sticks that the track-walker sent up after him.

This was the day following the "cloud-burst" under the water-tank: the morrow of the second night's watch. Little Jack, thoroughly exhausted, was sleeping like a weary soldier, regardless of mosquitoes, heat, ticks, and red-ants. Tommy had filled the tank long before the sun came up over the tree-tops. The engineers, having heard of the struggles and hardships of the young railroaders, were taking water at Highland and Hagler's whenever it was possible to do so, in order to save the water at Silver Creek.

The stationary engineer at Highland and the mule at Hagler's kicked, but it did no good. The sympathy of the whole division was with the agent's *protégé* at the tank, and the sad-faced little watchman in the red shanty down by the river.

Tommy and Mary waited dinner for nearly an hour under the old elm that day.

They waited until Tommy declared that he

could eat his whiskers, if he had any to eat, and Jack was still asleep. At two o'clock the watchman came out, bathed his mosquito-bitten face in the river, had dinner — what was left of it — and declared himself ready to relieve his companion. But Tommy would not go to sleep. He flagged a work-train and went up to St. Jacobs.

"I want yo' to write a request to the road-master," said Tommy.

"Ah! Tommy," said the agent, "a requisition for supplies so soon?"

"Well, things got t' be fixed up a little down there 'f we stay on d' job."

"The Lord loveth a cheerful kicker," said the agent, looking down upon his young friend. Seeing the agent with pen in hand, Tommy led off, —

"Screen door, an' skeeter bar on d' winder."

The agent wrote it as nearly as possible as Tommy gave the order.

"That's so Jack kin sleep daytime," he explained.

"Very well."

"'Nother stool fur d' table. That's fur Mary — but yo' need'n say so. She brings d' dinner, an' she's got a' eat same as men."

"Yes."

"New giers fur d' mule, an' scissors to cut his mane an' tail."

"Yes."

"New oil can. De mule stepped on d' ol' one — but you need'n put that in d' letter — tings is s'posed to wear out sometime."

"Very well."

"Red flag an' white flag, red globe an' a white globe. Them's fur extras."

"Is that all?"

"No. Five gallons signal oil. Might's well git enough while we're at it."

"Yes, Tommy," said the agent, "but you must remember that all these supplies will be charged up to you, and your reign at the river will be successful or otherwise in proportion to the expense of the station."

"I don't quite git yeh," said Tommy, eyeing the agent. "Yo' don't think fur a secont 'at I'm goin' t' put up fur this truck?"

"Not exactly, Tommy; but the company

holds you responsible for the property in your charge, and you must be as economical — that is, as saving — as if you were paying for them."

Tommy looked troubled.

"Do you think you really need all these things?" asked the station-master.

"Yes," said Tommy, positively. He was usually positive, one way or the other.

"Anything else?"

"Well," said Tommy, thoughtfully, "they ort 'o be a 'Merican flag top 'o d' tank an' d' fort."

"The company does n't furnish fireworks or prepared patriotism for its employees, Tommy, you know," said the agent, looking seriously at the ambitious young official.

"Well, jist say, after th' flag business, 'at your deescrishunt or something 'at 'ill show they don't haf t' fill that order," said Tommy, nodding his head to indicate his perfect satisfaction with himself.

CHAPTER VI

THEY HOIST THE FLAG

WHEN the Highland accommodation stopped for water, about a week after Tommy had received the supplies which he had requested, the express messenger kicked off a long bundle marked " Tent, West Silver Creek Bridge. (D. H.)"

When the train pulled out a couple of Mr. Collins's men climbed up the water tank. After sighting and measuring for a while the men came down and asked : " Where's your flag ? "

" We aint go' no flag," said the pump boy.

" Well, we've been sent here to put up a flag. What's in that bundle ? "

" Tent ! " yelled Tommy, after examining the tag. " Hully smoke, Jack, we're goin' t' have a tent," cried he, enthusiastically, as he began to cut the twine about the bundle. Tommy's eyes widened when he shook the bundle open and found a big silk banner wearing the stars and stripes. " D' flag ! d' flag,

Jack!" he cried excitedly, as he threw the little watchman down and began to roll him up in the silk that lay upon the grass.

The company storekeeper had run a blue pencil through the flag in Tommy's requisition, and then headed a subscription to buy what the boy wanted. Every trainman on the division, agents, operators, section men — in fact, all who heard of the thing, were eager to contribute, so that the best and biggest flag that could be bought and used in such a place, took less than half the money. The balance was spent for red fire and noise, so that the boys at the bridge, who never knew what it was to have a holiday — who knew it was Sunday once a week because the Highland local did n't run — could amuse themselves and the people of Lick Skillet without losing any time.

The following day was the Fourth, and the first train up from St. Louis brought the fireworks. It was a great day; the biggest in the history of the settlement, and Tommy McGuire, who had been stoned and chased, freckled Tommy, "Onry Tommy," whom the priest called "incourageable," who had been voted a thoroughly worthless boy by all the females in the community — save his mother and little Mary — was easily the captain. And what pleased the agent, Tommy's champion, who had driven down to the Skillet to see the show, was the fact that Tommy wore his honors easily. There was nothing of the swaggerer about him. To be sure, he awed the other boys, especially the farmer boys from a little way back, and he held the eyes of all the little girls, who envied Mary Connor, who was ever near the master of ceremonies, partly because she felt a sort of security in his company and partly from force of habit, for they were constant companions now. This fact did not escape the notice of the agent. It was a good sign, he said, to see a boy throwing a line out early in life.

Once, when the big flag had become entangled about the pole, Tommy ran up the pump ladder and over the roof of the tank to loosen it. Then, to save time, he slid down a long rope that reached from the roof to within ten feet of the ground. Every one was watching the boy, and when he dropped Mary put her hands to her eyes and said, "Oh!" and then she blushed and all the other girls laughed.

The station agent, who, instead of going to St. Louis to celebrate, had complimented the community by his presence, was, by common consent, the guest of honor. The section men brought a push-car load of lumber and built a big table, upon which the Widow Connor and Mrs. McGuire heaped the best products of their well-worked gardens. There was spring chicken, butter, and buttermilk. The agent stood at the head of the table, Tommy at his right, and little Mary, by a mere accident, at his left. In addition to keeping one eye on the agent and the other on Mary, Tommy looked out for every one. He was especially solicitous for Mrs. Dutton, who had given him the name of "Onry" Tommy, and saw that her plate was kept loaded. He even expressed a regret that the priest could not be there "to git a square once in his life."

By the middle of the afternoon the news of the "celebration" at the bridge had filtered out among the farmers and reached up to St. Jacobs and down to Troy, and those who had made no arrangements to enjoy the Fourth, came to the water tank that evening to see the fireworks. Tommy had caused the section men to lay boards along one side of the bridge, and when it was dark, having the multitude, to the number of two or three hundred souls, including "Anderson's nigger," stationed at a distance, he stood upon the bridge and burned money. If he had dazzled the youth of the community, male and female, by day, he awed them at night. Standing there on the bridge in a blaze of glory, with Mary by his side, making it thunder and lighten, sending sizzling sky-rockets over the tops of tall trees, shooting burning bullets into the blue above, Tommy McGuire was easily the emperor of Lick Skillet, grand, picturesque, and awful.

CHAPTER VII

THE LABOR QUESTION

"SAY, Jack, d' roadmaster won't know this mule," said Tommy, standing off and looking the animal over. "Mr. Heidelberg says they's just one thing 'at looks onryer 'n a long-haired mule, 'at's a short-haired woman. Women an' horses should be trimmed alike, an' men an' mules."

With that Tommy put away his clippers and started the mule on his circular journey. The ingenious pump boy had grown tired of the narrow platform in the centre of the circle and conceived the idea of bringing a camp stool and sitting in the shadow of a tree just outside the ring. Immediately the mule walked to the far side of the circle and stopped. Tommy whipped him around the ring and tried it again. The mule stopped. Now up to this point it had made no great difference where the boy sat, but he would conquer the mule. He made a blind for the mule's off eye, so that he could not see the driver as he went past, but, to his surprise, on the other side of the circle it was the near eye the mule used. He changed it. The mule went around to where he had been stopping, stopped, turned his head until his open eye was brought to bear upon his master, gave a deep sigh, and settled down to rest. Tommy was angry. He now put a blind over both the mule's eyes, and the animal refused to budge. Tommy gave him a few sharp cracks and gave it up. He thought on the matter a great deal. It was the first time he had failed utterly; the first time he had ever been conquered; and by a mule! It was humiliating. He made a dummy and set it where he had been sitting, started the mule going and dodged behind a sycamore near where the mule was wont to stop. The animal pulled round to the effigy, shied a little, came nearer, smelled of it. snorted, and then began coolly to eat the stuffing out of it — some wisps of hay that were sticking up out of the dummy's collar.

Little Jack came over, saw the dummy, and asked what it was for. Tommy was loath to acknowledge his defeat, and now a new idea came into his head. "We'll stan' that dummy at d' end of d' bridge, hang a white light on his arm an' let d' Midnight Express go by while we sleep, eh! Jack, old boy?"

Jack smiled.

"An' say, Jack! d' you know we can give d' dummy a lamp fur d' Midnight Express an' a flag for the White Mail in d' morning an' sleep till sun up."

"An' the red light," Jack began, "how we goin' t' fix that, Tommy? S'posen the dummy wants a red light?"

"Thatso," said Tommy. "An' say, Jack," he added quickly, "spose d' bridge ketch afire, is d' dummy gun to put it out? Jimminy!" and with that Tommy made a run at his dummy, hit him a kick in the ribs, dragged him to the bank, and without more ado sent him down to a watery grave.

"That's a good lesson for you, Mr. Jack Connor," said Tommy, taking the whip and climbing up on the platform. "Do yer work yerself an' hold yer job, an' don't depend on d' Union. They's too much machinery already in th' worl'. U. P. says the inventor's robbin' d' workin' man. Here we 've both got good jobs an' we 're tryin' to make a dummy watch a bridge."

Jack was thoroughly shamed.

"Aint you got sense nuff to know, Jack Connor, that if a dummy 'd do, the company 'd have a dummy 'stead o' payin' you forty dollars a month to stay here?"

Jack nodded his head. "Spose you made a dummy an' it done d' work, long comes Mr. Roadmaster, sees d' dummy, says 'that's a good thing,' an' you git d' bounce. No, sir, when a fellow 's got a job he wants to hold it, an' not go sawin' it off on an effigy, same as soldiers 'at 's grafted in d' war an 's afraid to fight. There 's a good lesson fur you, Mr. Jack," added Tommy: "Hold yer job an' don't bank on d' Union or a dummy;" and with this advice Tommy cracked the mule up and subsided, with a countenance fixed and resolute.

CHAPTER VIII

LITTLE JACK'S PROMOTION

"I DON'T care a tinker's dime about Denis McGuire," said the agent, angrily, "but something must be done for little Jack. He's having malaria. Winter will be coming on and he can't stand a winter in that shanty."

"I can take Jack in my office to carry dispatches," said the roadmaster; "but who can I put on the bridge to watch it as that boy does?"

"There you are," replied the agent, sarcastically. "Because the boy is faithful, you would keep him there until he dies and leaves his mother utterly helpless. But," he added quickly — for he was a good stayer when he elected to stay — "since you ask my advice, I'll tell you: Put Denis McGuire on the bridge — he's a cripple for life; crippled in the service of this company."

"I've told ye," said the roadmaster, "that

Denis McGuire was barred from workin' fur the Vandalia phile I 'm here."

The agent wore a look of disgust, as he turned to answer a call.

Presently he came near the roadmaster, drew a chair, and said, as though he were telling a new, strange story to a little child: "I knew a section boss once who let a flat car get away on the hill at Collinsville; the car ran out on the main line, collided with the President's private car, wrecked it and killed a trainman. He was discharged, reinstated after a few months, and is now — "

"That was not my fault," broke in the roadmaster, "I sint a man to set the brake."

"Denis McGuire sent a man to flag, but — "

"And he should have seen the flagman beyent th' curve before loadin' th' push kayre."

"And the gentleman at Collinsville should have seen that the brake was in working order before kicking the block from under the wheel with his own brave foot," said the agent, nodding his head to clinch the point.

The roadmaster was beaten out. Presently he got to his feet and began walking the floor.

When the local freight came along the agent told the conductor what had passed between the official and himself. "Hazelton," said the agent, "they won't give you a passenger train because you're a good man on freight. Jim Law is no good as a freight man so they reward him with a soft run; a thorn for virtue and a rose for vice. Hazelton, the poor should help the poor — speak a word for little Jack, the Hibernian czar goes down with you to-day."

And it came to pass that Denis McGuire, with one leg shorter than the other, was made watchman at Silver Creek, and little Jack went to be messenger boy in the office of the road-master.

Although loath to part company with his little friend, Tommy rejoiced at Jack's good luck. What distressed him most was the thought that little Mary would not come now to fetch his dinner and put fresh flowers in the old tomato can.

There was no need for him to stay in the shanty nights; in fact, his mother wanted his protection, so Tommy moved back to the McGuire cottage in the heart of Lick Skillet.

To his surprise, Mary continued to bring his dinner until the beginning of the winter term of school, after which Tommy ate a cold lunch or came home for his dinner. He invariably had the tank filled, his mule stabled, and was up the road to meet Mary on her way from school. In winter, when the snow was deep, he took the mule, and the sled that Mr. Collins had made for him, and brought Mary home. It was wonderful, the change that had come over this apparently worthless boy within a year. He could walk into the pay-car, sign his name for forty dollars, and it was his, and he was a man, all but the whiskers, and he felt sure that they would be along on time.

When Jack came home for the holidays, with a new suit of store clothes, presents for his mother, a new, warm cloak for Mary, and firecrackers for all the little boys in the place, he and Tommy had many a happy hour together. East St. Louis was a wonderful city, and they were building a great bridge across the river that ran between the two towns, as wide as Anderson's orchard and as deep as a well. And some day the roadmaster was going to give Tommy a lay-off and he was to visit Jack, and they would cross the great river on a steamboat with a whistle as big as the water tank.

"An' dive off d' bridge," broke in Tommy, enthusiastically.

CHAPTER IX

TOMMY FLAGS THE WHITE MAIL

AT last the long winter broke, spring came back, the grass grew green upon the graves of the old watchman and his son, school was out, and little Mary brought Tommy's dinner, as she had done the summer before.

When seven o'clock came of a morning, Denis McGuire would limp home and Tommy would ride his mule down the track behind the White Mail.

It had been raining for nearly a week, the fields were flooded and the trains late.

Half of East St. Louis was under water, and the broad bottoms, seen from Collinsville, looked like a vast ocean. For twenty-four hours both East and West Silver Creek had been rising rapidly. An extra, taking water at the tank, told McGuire that the mail was an hour late at Effingham, and McGuire went home, leaving the bridge in Tommy's care. Whilst he was walking home and the boy was riding down (the mule went fearfully slow to work), the water was rising fast. As Tommy came near the bridge he noticed that the water, in places, was almost up to the ends of the ties. Below the track it was two feet lower, and the boy sat watching the boiling flood of black water that was sucking under the bridge. Occasionally great logs would strike against the wooden piling and shake the whole structure. Tommy was thoroughly alarmed — not for himself — for he believed himself capable of swimming the widest river that ran, but for the White Mail that would soon come over the ridge and down the short hill like falling down a well. Suddenly, a great elm tree that stood near the bank above the bridge toppled over into the stream, drifted crosswise against the bridge and lodged.

The roots and branches of the huge tree choked the channel, other trees and logs drifted against it, and a great wall of water began to rise rapidly above the track. Finding the outlet clogged, the river ran swiftly along the railway, east and west, until it came to the bluffs. It backed up far into the forest over the flat bottoms, grew higher and heavier, and the old bridge began to tremble. Meanwhile the fresh engine that had taken the White Mail that morning at Effingham was quivering across the great prairies of Illinois. Pausing to quench her thirst at Highlands she dashed away again and was now whistling for St. Jacobs. A drunken little Dutch tailor, who had boarded the train at the last stop, insisted upon getting off at St. Jacobs.

"The next stop is East St. Louis," said Conductor Wise, punching his ticket.

"Vell, eef you sthop or nit, I git off ust de same," and, as the train whistled, a quarter of a mile above the station, the fool Dutchman stepped out into space and came down on the east end of the platform.

The agent, standing in front of the station (it was a sight to see the White Mail go by an hour late), saw a bundle of old clothes come rolling swiftly down the long platform, and finally fetch up with a bump against the end of the depot. The Dutchman was in that bundle. In all the history of the Vandalia Line the greatest marvel is that this man lived;

that he actually got up and asked the agent to have a glass of beer. So, if there is ever a proper time for a man to become hopelessly and helplessly inebriated, it would seem to be just before getting off a mail train onto a hardwood platform at a mile a minute.

About the time the Dutchman hit the earth, the old bridge began to tremble and crack, like the breaking up of a hard winter. A moment later the great stringers parted, the river, laden with logs and trees, rushed into the opening, and the bridge was gone.

Even as Tommy turned his mule the water was running across the track between the ties. The mule, gladdened by the prospect of avoiding the pump and getting back to the stable, trotted briskly away, and finally, by dint of much kicking and thumping, broke into a run.

Tommy knew that the White Mail was almost due, and that if he failed to gain the ridge before she pitched over, she must leap into that awful flood, with all on board. He knew the old engineer, and how he ran when the Mail was late. He thought of the newsboy, now a flagman, who had given him picture papers, of Conductor Wise and his pretty daughter — almost as pretty as Mary.

When he came to the road-crossing where they usually turned off, the mule stopped. Tommy reined him to the track again and urged him on. He could almost see over the ridge, but not quite. A heavy mist was rising from the wet earth, filling the wood with gray fog. The boy glanced back, but could see nothing. The roar of the river, pouring over the grade, grew louder, instead of fainter, as he rode away.

Suddenly the White Mail screamed on the ridge, not a thousand feet from the mule. Instantly Tommy reined him over the rail, waving his straw hat in lieu of a flag. The mule moved slowly, showing contempt for the train. Until now, Tommy had not thought of his own life. He felt that the train would stop — must stop. Peering from his window, the old engineer saw something on the track, and instantly felt like hitting it, for was he not already nearly an hour late? He would not shut off. A second glance showed him the rider, dimly through the gray mist. Now he saw the hat and recognized the pump boy. The old man's heart stood still as he shoved the throttle home, but it was too late, and Tommy and the mule went out of the right-of-way.

Denis McGuire had seen the engine strike the boy and hurried to him where he lay.

His mother came, and presently many of the neighbors, the trainmen, and some of the passengers. His mother lifted his head and held it in her lap.

They brought some water from the car and threw it in his face, and he came to life again. The men put money in his old straw hat; the women kissed him; for the train had stopped with the nose of the engine at the water-edge. After casting a pitying glance at the remains of the old mule, Tommy went away, walking wabbly, between little Mary and his mother.

CHAPTER X

TOMMY McGUIRE SEES THE CITY

IT took Tommy McGuire more than a month to recover from the effect of his head-end collision with the White Mail. The old pump mule, upon whose back Tommy had hurried to the top of the hill in the face of the flying train, had lost his life, and the railway company had lost a mule, but the company made no complaint. The brave boy, by warning the engineer, had saved the company the trouble and expense of hauling a heavy engine from the bottom of a very muddy stream, rebuilding a number of cars, and apologizing to the postal authorities at Washington, to say nothing of costly damage suits. And the President of the Vandalia had marked the pump boy at West Silver Creek for promotion. He had issued orders to that effect to his subordinate officials. All these interesting facts had been made known to Tommy by little Mary Connor, who had it by letter from her brother Jack, the messenger boy in the office of the roadmaster at East St. Louis.

It had been arranged that Tommy should visit his friend, little Jack, at the river, as soon as he was able to travel, and to that visit the pump boy looked forward with great expectations.

It was mid-summer when Tommy boarded the Highland accommodation one morning at St. Jacobs. Heidelberg, the agent, had consigned him to the care of the conductor, for none thought of transportation for Tommy McGuire, the hero of Silver Creek. Jack met him at the depot at East St. Louis and took him at once to his boarding house. After dinner the messenger boy, who had been in the great city for nearly a year, allowed Tommy to accompany him on his rounds among the various departments of the road.

Tommy was surprised to see the timid Jack pushing his way through crowds, darting across the tracks between the snorting switch engines, talking back to the big policemen, and even threatening to thump a grocer's boy who was trying to run them down.

After supper that evening the boys took a ferry and crossed the great river. Tommy, who had found little to awe him in his short life, said, looking over-side, that it was awful. As they neared the west bank the noise of the heavy traffic along the river front became deafening. As far as they could see, up and down the river, there was nothing but houses, and high above their heads hung the skeleton of the big bridge. Tommy breathed easier when he felt the flagging beneath his feet. He was inclined to shrink from the big wagons and heavy drays that rattled past them in the narrow street, but when he caught little Jack grinning at him, he determined to face whatever came without flinching. A boy who had once ridden a mule up against an express train ought not to be afraid of a dray, or a thousand drays.

When they had wandered for an hour, never losing sight of the river that showed through the narrow streets up as far as Broadway, Jack bethought him of the spending-money the roadmaster had given him. Presently, near the door of a little wooden shop, they saw a sign that read:

"Sweet Cider and Cigars."

They were too big for candy, and not big enough for beer, so Jack thought the sweet cider sign about the proper thing.

There was no light in the place, save the little that filtered through the dirty window and fell from the street lamp through the open door.

The boys hesitated, but when the voice of a woman called kindly to them, bidding them enter, they stepped inside. Jack called for cider, and when they had tasted it they both said it was not cider. They refused to drink it, but both pulled out their pocket books and wanted to pay. They had each put a quarter on the little showcase and the woman took both. The boys waited in silence for their change, and the silence was broken by the snoring of a man just behind the calico curtains that cut the narrow room eight feet from the door.

"Won't yez have some candy, boys?" asked the woman, sliding the door in the show-case and putting in a fat hand.

"No!" said Jack; "we want our change."

"Yez don't git no change. Drinks is twenty-five cents in this shop."

"Come on! les go," said Tommy.

"No, yez don't," said the woman, stepping from behind the low counter and pushing the door shut. "Yez'll drink what yez ordered or I'll call th' police."

The boys glanced at each other. Jack was thoroughly frightened. Tommy was fighting mad. "Open that door," he demanded. The woman laughed, a laugh that the boys had never heard before, locked the door and removed the key.

Tommy was about to throw himself upon her as she stepped toward the curtains, but Jack caught hold of his arm.

"Moik! Moik! I say Moik, wake up. Come ahn, ye brute, git up."

The woman passed behind the curtains and was endeavoring to rouse the sleeping man. The place was quite dark now, with the door shut. The narrow window panes were covered with dust, and only a faint ray struggled through from a street lamp.

Tommy tried the door. "Take hold of my

shoulder," said he to Jack, "and pull for your life."

Tommy grasped the knob, put one foot against the door jamb, and the two scared boys threw themselves back with all the strength they had. The screws that held the lock in place must have been eaten with rust, or the wood rotten, for the door gave way and the boys fell backward into the room.

As they scrambled to their feet and rushed out, the woman came after them, calling: "Police! police!" but the boys kept on running. They turned a corner and made for the river. Once or twice they thought they heard the heavy boots of a policeman close behind them, but they never looked back. They reached the river just as a ferry-boat was about to pull in the plank, and leaped aboard.

When they had gained courage to look back they saw a policeman standing on the wharf looking at the boat. No doubt he was looking at them, and they went forward, their hearts still beating wildly when they stepped ashore on the Illinois side.

"Les go home," said Tommy.

"Never. Everybody in St. Louis knows me, and if we 've been reco'nized they 'll go right to the house to git us. We must not go home to-night."

"Well, les don't stan' here where they can see us," said Tommy, and they strolled down along the water-edge.

They climbed up onto an old, abandoned cart and watched the ferry-boats come and go. They watched closely for the caps and buttons of police officers among the passengers that passed out between the two big lamps on the landing.

"Like as not they 'll put on citizens' clothes, or maybe send detectives after us, an' you can't tell a detective from anybody else; sometimes they dress up like storekeepers an' sometimes like tramps."

It was quite dark now, where the boys sat upon the old cart, and presently they saw three men coming up the river, walking slowly and talking low.

"Come on," said Jack, grasping Tommy's arm, and hurrying down to the very water-edge. They hid under an old, abandoned wooden pier and waited for the men to pass by, for they made no doubt that they were detectives.

"They must have seen us," whispered Jack, "they're comin' out on the pier." Now the boys tried to hold their breath, for the men were walking silently over their hiding place, and not four feet above them.

The three men sat down upon one of the stringers that pointed out over the water.

"Hark! what's that?" said one.

"What's what? you idict; you're worse 'an a two-year-old, shyin' at a fallin' leaf."

"I heard someon' cough."

"It's that chicken heart of yours hittin' your vest. Close that fissure in your face."

"Aw, cheese it," said the third man, "what's on yer mind, Charley?"

"A whole lot," said the severe man, who seemed to be the captain. "The night express is the proper train, Monday night the time, and Casey Water-Tank the place."

Tommy hunched Jack.

"There's always a lot of mail and express matter that accumulates here over Sunday, therefore the Monday fast express ought to be good picking."

A bareheaded woman came down to the river, looked into the boiling flood, shivered and went away, manifestly determined to make one more effort to solve the bread and butter problem.

When she had passed out of hearing, the man went on: " Jim 'll go to Casey to-morrow, Sunday, and make his way to the tank. Having the only decent suit, I'll take a sleeper for Indianapolis, but I promise you I won't sleep. And Pete, you white-livered coyote, you 'll take the blind baggage at Greenup, so as to be on hand when the time comes."

"An' how do we proceed?" asked Jim.

"You 'll be hiding behind the tank, and when the fireman's wrestling with the spout an' the engineer's watching his signals so as to place the engine, you 'll step quietly aboard, holding your gun close to the engineer, but not offensively close so as to enable him to take it away from you."

"An' must I pint it butt fust, er nozzle fust? You know I hain't never handled a gun afore."

"Well, if you handle it as recklessly as you handle the English language you'll kill the man on sight. Well, to my tale: Pete will uncouple the train the moment the engineer has placed the engine and wait for me."

"An' what'll the great man do?" demanded Jim, who was feeling the insult to his grammar.

"The great man will herd the car-hands up through the sleepers and into the day coach, where he will proceed to pacify the passengers. Having slipped into his false face he will pause with his back to the door at the rear of the car, twirl his arsenal playfully, and bid the multitude be quiet. For the further awing of those who may meditate violence he will fire three shots — bang, bang, bang — that shall come like the measured thumping of my lady's heart, when she sees a cow. These pistol shots will be followed by the tinkling sound of falling glass, for the three glims will have been doused. And, by the same token you shall know, O, Jimmie, and you, my shivering Pete, that your uncle is doing business in the day coach."

"An' I'll come in wud a mail sack an' git de watches and diamins."

"Watches! shade of Jesse! Does Two-card Charley rob unarmed men and helpless women? You will devote your time and that mite of gray matter that you are supposed to have in your head to the parting of the train."

"S'pose some on' shows fight?"

"Why, apologize and bow yourself out, of course. Oh, Pete! Pete! I've tried to make something of you, but it isn't in the wood. It hurts me to hint such a thing, and yet I know the day will come when I must needs lay violent hands on you; kill you, mayhap, and cache you in the waving grass, you ass."

Pete had stuck a short pipe into his mouth, and now indiscreetly struck a parlor match and held it to the pipe. The intellectual leader struck the pipe and the match with his open hand and drove them into the face of Pete, and immediately the conference broke up.

The two boys lay quiet until the men had passed the big lamp at the landing, and then crawled out.

"Say, Jack," said Tommy, and the sound of his voice broke the silence so suddenly that Jack started and clutched at his friend's arm, "them fellows 'll be hidin' out same as us, if they don't watch out."

"Shall we tell on 'em?"

"Sure! Aint the company's business our business?"

"Yes; still we would n't like to have somebody tell on us."

"But what have we done, Jack Connor? We ordered the drinks an' paid for 'em — both of us."

"An' pulled the door down. You often hear of fellows bein' sent up for breakin' into houses."

"We did n't break in; we broke out, to gain our freedom. Liberty, Heidelberg says, is the rightful heritage of American citizens."

Now, the boys, full of a great tale, stole softly up the shadow side of the street, and to bed.

CHAPTER XI

THE HOLD-UP AT CASEY'S TANK

IT was Sunday in St. Louis, and in East St. Louis as well, but there was no rest for the officials of the Vandalia Line. Little Jack, the messenger boy, and Tommy, the pump boy, were being examined by the superintendent. The boys told their story without embarrassment. A boy who has been messenger for a year in the roadmaster's office, and another boy who has been up against the White Mail with his mule, when the Mail was making little less than a mile a minute, are not going to get rattled when telling a simple story. When the superintendent had heard that Two-card Charley, Jim, and Pete were going to rob the Midnight Express on Monday night, he began to work the wire that went to Chicago.

Then, as now, Chicago was the headquarters of the famous Watchem Detective Agency, and the Vandalia wanted a good detective, right away, regardless of expense.

Now, the elder Watchem happened to be a personal friend of the President of the Vandalia Line, and he would send none other than his boy, Billy, who had already made a world-wide reputation as a criminal catcher. But Billy was away chasing a bank robber through the Michigan forests, and could not be found.

Late in the afternoon the Superintendent grew impatient, but the head of the Chicago agency assured him that a detective would reach the river in time to take the Midnight Express on Monday night.

When the last train over the Alton left Chicago that Sunday night, with no detective on board, the Superintendent went swearing to bed. When all the morning trains pulled out on Monday, bringing no help, the Superintendent said, over the wire, to Watchem, that he would give the business to Theil. Whereupon, old man Watchem reached over to Indianapolis, touched the President, and the President said, over the wire, to the Superintendent, "Leave it all to Watchem," and he left it, and sulked in his tent the day.

The Michigan pines were making long shadows on Monday afternoon when Billy Watchem came to the lake-side and caught a wire from his father, bidding him hurry home.

"Step lively," said Billy to his burglar, "you're not the only robber on the road. There is work for me near the home office;" and so the men made haste.

The lamps had been lighted about the post office when young Watchem rushed into the office of the Chicago & Alton and asked for a special engine to carry him to East St. Louis. In his haste he got on the wrong spur, and stumbled over a little, inexpensive, but extremely officious official, whose business it is to pass upon the credentials of country editors and see that the company's advertisements are properly printed.

"For whom do you want a special?" asked the keeper of the clippings.

"For myself; that's 'whom.'"

Now, the keeper of the clippings gave the young man one withering glance, and turned away with a hauteur in the presence of which the President would have paled, as the morning star pales before the rising sun.

At that moment a comfortable looking man stepped from the elevator. That was the little man's chief.

"Hello, Billy," said the General Passenger Agent, giving the young detective a glad hand, "are you all packed?"

"All packed," said Billy, glancing at a hand grip that till now had been hidden beneath a fall overcoat that hung on his arm.

"Then let us be off. We've got a special engine and Pullman car waiting at the station for you," and the two men went down together.

"Now, have I made of myself an ass?" mused the keeper of the clippings. "I would have wagered my position that he was the editor of the Litchfield Lamplight, and he goes to the river by special train over our road. Ay, over the Alton," and he closed his desk with a bang.

"I want you to make a mile a minute to-night," said the General Passenger Agent, offering a cigar to the engineer, as the slim eight-wheeler moved out of the station shed.

As the car clicked over the switches, the young detective turned to a cold lunch that the black boy had builded in the buffet, for he had not eaten since morning. He had scarcely commenced his meal when the heavy sleeper began to slam her flanges up against the rail and show him that she was rolling. The Alton was one of the oldest of the western roads, and upon this occasion she would take her place as pace-maker for the rest, just as she had taught the Atlantic lines the use of sleeping and dining cars. Indeed it is here, upon these very rails, that we are wont to picture young Mr. Pullman, with a single blanket and a wisp broom, swinging himself into his first sleeper, that was not his, but a rented car.

By the time young Watchem had finished his "tea" the roar of passing towns was coming closer and closer together. When the flying engine screamed for a crossing, the whistle sounded above his head, and far away in the rear of his car a rain of fire was falling in the furrowed fields.

As well might the engine have been running light, for the one sleeper only served to steady her. She was making a mile on a shovel of coal, and five posts on a single fire.

"What's that?"

"Lexington," said the porter, bracing himself with a hand on a seat at either side of the aisle. "I tell you, boss, we're flyin'. Dey don' mak' no swiftah ingin dan de nine-spot; an' ef yo' heah me shout, dat man Jim know how t' hit 'er, too."

"What's that?"

"Bloomin'ton, sah. I tell you, boss, dese towns am brushin' by de windahs to-night lak telegraph poles — we're flyin', boss, — flyin', da's all."

At a station where they took water, the dispatcher asked the engineer if he could stand the strain to cover the entire route. They were holding the Midnight Express at the river. This was the most important train on the Van. "Tell him yes," said the engineer to the operator, as he opened the throttle. The Alton was making history.

"We're goin' through, Mickey," shouted the engineer, holding his open watch in the thin glare of light that shot up behind the furnace door that was on the latch.

"Good!" said the fireman, catching the enthusiasm that was contagious in the cab.

When the two men had worked so, nervously alert, for another hour, they were drunk with the excitement of the trip. They could not talk for the roar and roll of the engine, but they could see each other in the dim light, and smile at each other across the cab.

As tank after tank they passed without stopping, the fireman would look over at the engineer, and the driver, making the sign of a man drinking (which means "water" on an engine), would jerk his thumb over his shoulder, and the fireman would go back and sound the engine tank and show the wet line on the shovel handle to the engineer, and he would raise his right hand and wriggle his wrist, which means "All right, let 'er go."

Then he would take off his cap, hold his head out of the cab window, and cool his temples in the dewy twilight. He had no thought now of danger; not the faintest appreciation of the risk he was running. He would drive her so to the very edge of the Mississippi, and, if the lights were white, and the switches right, and if it were necessary, he would take the trackless, tieless skeleton of the big bridge that was being built over the broad river. They were flying.

The President of the C. & A., by a singular coincidence, was watching at the Columbia Theatre in Chicago, men and women going 'round the world in eighty days. "This," thought the railway man, "is play-acting, and you can't prove it. But this," he would add, as message after message was passed into his box, "this play that the Alton is putting up tonight is the real thing."

The Midnight Express was thirty minutes overdue to leave when the driver of the special, pale but calm faced, dashed up to the station at East St. Louis and brought them to a stand with an emergency stop.

"This is no boy's business," growled the Superintendent, as he hurried the young man from the special to the rear of the Midnight Express. "Where's your father?"

"In Chicago. Got any instructions?"

The Superintendent handed the voyager an envelope containing a letter, his transportation, and a check for an upper berth.

"Thank you," said the young man, and,

ignoring the insult to his tender age, he swung himself into one of the sleepers that were gliding by.

Side by side with the Midnight Express came the O. & M. broad gauge, lumbering along, her high wheels climbing the cold steel rails that lay in "splendid isolation," with six feet of earth between them. The O. & M. Cannon Ball was jealous of the Midnight Express. In fact it was the coming of the new line, with her narrower, swifter engines, that caused the rails of the O. & M. to get together on a sensible gauge, that has since become a standard for American railways. Side by side the two trains passed the last lights of the city, and found the open fields. Of course there would be a race. Everybody knew that, and when the big engine had got her short train well under way, and her smoke lay across the Van Line in the glare of the light of the Midnight Express, she whistled the other man ahead. Under these circumstances that constitutes a "dare," and no self-respecting engineer will take it. The Van answered the signal. The Express was a heavy train, and before the driver could get them going (he would not tear the fireman's fire, full of green coal) he was looking into the tail lights of the Cannon Ball. Five miles out the broad gauge had reached the limit of her speed. The black plunger at the head of the Night Express was hanging at her flank, as you have seen a farm-dog hang at the side of a sow, racing up through a field, with only a row of corn between them. Gradually she began to gain. To the joy of her driver and all of her passengers, she began to crawl up. Her headlight could no longer be seen from the sleepers behind the Cannon Ball — only the glare of it. Now her stack stood opposite the mail car on the O. & M. She would soon have the sow by the ear. There was not a man, woman, or child on either of the two trains that did not enter into the excitement of the chase. Now the headlight of the broad gauge engine shone full on the face of the daring driver of the Midnight Express, who was looking back from the cab window. He whistled the man ahead, and a moment later the Van flyer, swinging into a shallow cañon near Collinsville, showed her tail lights to the Cannon Ball.

Of all the people on the two trains, the man who was to occupy lower seven and the man who was to occupy upper seven were least interested in the race. The former kept his thin face, with its receding forehead, pressed to the pane, peering into the night, and thinking wild and awful thoughts.

"What are these common carriers but soulless corporations, oppressors of the poor,— the poor that are growing poorer, as the rich grow richer. Something is radically wrong. The world owes me a living and I mean to have it."

These and many other thoughts were running through the young man's almost empty head. Beside him lay a copy of the "Police Gazette" and a small yellow-back branded "Dead on the Desert;" and when young Watchem, who held a check for upper seven, saw the literature, he guessed that this must be Two-card Charley, the amateur and somewhat theatrical young highwayman. Noting the almost expressionless face and the nothingness of the man's physique, the strong young detective felt sympathy for this would-be criminal.

Retiring to the smoking-room the detective read his letter of instructions, which was little more and no less than the story of how the messenger boy and the pump boy had overheard the three conspirators conspiring to rob the Midnight Express. In Pete, the chicken-hearted, the shrewd detective recognized "Epsom Pete," who had held up a stenographer and burglarized a box car in Kansas City. Of Two-card Charley he knew nothing, save the little he had gathered from a few moments' observation. To begin with, Charley smoked cigarettes excessively, and that made him wakeful and nervous. He ate opium, and that wrecked his morals. But Jim — "Cheyenne Jim," as he called himself — was a hard nut. His knife-handle, as Watchem was well aware, was notched for two Chinamen, a sheriff, and a Sioux. He was a coward. All his men had been killed going, and a conscienceless coward had no business with a gun. This man must be handled gingerly or somebody would get hurt.

Presently Charley came and sat in the narrow smoking-room opposite the detective, but with his gaze bent upon the black window.

"Charley," said Watchem, puffing at a cigar which he was attempting to re-light, and instantly Charley's right hand went back toward his pistol pocket, "we're going to have a hard winter, I think," he added, between puffs.

"Sir," exclaimed the robber, bringing his hands in front of him again, "you have me at some disadvantage."

"Oh, no! but I'd like to have you so; s'pose you give me your gun."

Again Charley's hand went back and his face went chalk white.

"Not so fast, not so fast, my boy," said the detective, shoving the point of his own pistol up to Charley's chin; "slowly now. That's it, butt first. Now we can talk."

But Charley only glared at the detective and refused to say a word. He had read in the various "works," with which he was more or less familiar, that the real game robber never gave up to a detective.

When the fresh locomotive that had been

hooked on at Effingham had galloped over the Ambraw bridge and stopped at Greenup, Epsom Pete boarded the blind baggage, and a moment later the black steed, snorting in the frosty morn, was dashing away across Fanchers' farm.

The detective took a pair of handcuffs, which he happened to have in his grip, and festooned them upon Charley's wrists. Stepping out on the rear platform he cut off a few feet of surplus bell rope that hung on the railing, and fettered Charley's feet, so that he might not jump off and lose himself.

When the engineer whistled for Casey Tank he cut the cord and marched the robber-chief up through the train. When the engine had been placed, the detective, standing on the rear end of the day coach, fired three shots, imitating as well as he knew how "the measured beating of my lady's heart."

Leaping to the ground, he pushed Charley along in front of him until they came to Pete, cutting the coupling. "Come on, Pete," said Watchem, and Pete, wondering who the new captain could be, followed on to the locomotive.

"Speak to the gentleman on the engine,

Charley," said the detective. "Call him off or I shall be compelled to kill him."

"Jim," said Charley, dramatically, "we have been betrayed. This train is loaded down with detectives and deputy sheriffs. We are surrounded, drop your gun."

"Just hand it over to the engineer, please," said Watchem. "There, that's better. There's not so many of me that I feel like fighting the whole band."

"An' now," said Pete, facing Two-card Charley, "I reckon here's whar' we 'pologize an' bow ourselves out."

CHAPTER XII

McGUIRE GOES WEST

HAVING saved the White Mail from a watery grave in the washout at West Silver Creek, and having also been instrumental in preventing the robbery of the Midnight Express at Casey's Tank, Tommy McGuire, the pump boy, was the most celebrated employee in the service of the Vandalia Line. The head of the average boy would have been turned with so much attention, but Tommy had inherited the democratic simplicity of his plain parents, and, with the exception of a scarcely perceptible throwing out of his chest, there was no apparent change in his mien when he stepped from the train at St. Jacobs after his eventful visit to East St. Louis. His mother had come up from the bridge to meet him.

"Ah, Tommy, darlint," she cried, clasping the boy in her arms, "they do be afther makin' a regular little jude uv ye, so they do, so they do."

Tommy kissed his mother, and put her from him as though she had been a child. He straightened his hat, that had been displaced, buttoned the top button on his store coat, and offered his hand to the agent, who now came forward to congratulate the young hero. It is to the boy's credit that he invariably colored a little when complimented upon his heroism in preventing the Casey robbery. He could not help recalling the fact that he was himself hiding from the police when he overheard the desperadoes planning to hold up the train. To be sure, he and his friend, little Jack, had committed no offence, but they thought they had.

Tommy had been home but a few days when he was ordered to report to the President of the road at Indianapolis. The President was favorably impressed by the boy's modesty. He sent him to the General Passenger Agent, who, finding that Tommy could read fairly well, set him reading the newspapers, clipping out and pasting on a broad piece of cardboard the daily comments of the press upon the road and its management. Upon another card he pasted the market and stock reports, and upon still another the railway news of the day, the name of the paper from which the cutting came being written at the bottom of each item. All this was for the convenience of busy officials. Tommy was greatly interested in his new work, and in a little while became expert. When he opened a newspaper his eye swept the page, and if there were a cap. "V" or an "R" he would catch it almost instantly and read what was said of the Vandalia or of railroads in general. There is no work in the passenger department of a railroad that does not sharpen the intellect and quicken the eye. The office of the General Passenger Agent is a school of itself, and a boy beginning with a very limited education will come out of such an office in a few years with an edge on him that would let him pass for at least a high school graduate. Tommy read constantly. He read the advertisements of the Vandalia and of other roads as well, and made comparisons. He ventured one day to call the attention of the Assistant General Passenger Agent to the plain, prosy unattractiveness of the company's advertising matter. He showed the ads. of a number of other lines, and famous soap display ads., and suggested a picture of the White Mail. The cut was made and proved very attractive, for the reason that nobody had ever seen a train of white cars in print before.

The editorial page of a New York daily, famous then as now for its clean type and clean English, attracted the boy's notice, and he read it religiously every day. The General Passenger Agent remembered distinctly that the boy had declared with characteristic frankness at their first meeting that he "did n't know nothing about the passenger business."

He noticed that the young man's form of speech had undergone a wonderful change. This was due to the fact that Tommy McGuire was remarkably observing. His daily intercourse was with the higher clerks and officials of the road. These men were his teachers, — these and the great editor in Nassau Street, whom he had never seen.

When winter and the dull times came, the General Passenger Agent persuaded Tommy to go to school. He objected to losing so much time, but, when assured that he could have his old place back in the spring, with an increase of pay, he consented. He attended a little college for boys, in St. Louis.

Tommy was as industrious in school as he had been in the office, and came back to his desk much improved. For three years he attended school in winter and worked in the office of the General Passenger Agent in summer. He was no longer the office boy, but the "Advertising Manager" for the passenger department of the line.

His friend, little Jack, having outgrown the clothes of a messenger boy, was now braking on a through passenger run, and so the boys renewed their acquaintance. Jack was also a great reader. His leisure hours were devoted to the study of the labor problem. He was much worried over the prospects of the workingman. He was one of those good, misguided souls who are ever on the alert for a grievance. Peace appeared to trouble his mind. "But what's the good of it all?" Tommy would ask.

"Mutual protection to elevate the general tone of the workingman."

"But, if everybody works and succeeds, we'll

all be at the front, Jack, old boy. My notion is that a great deal depends upon individual effort."

But Jack would not be comforted. He gave so much time and thought to his brother brakemen that he neglected his own job. He would forget his flags, and one night went out on the Midnight Express with no oil in his lamps. He had been reported by the conductor, but the trainmaster, knowing the sad history of his family, let him off with a sharp lecture. But a man in train service must have his mind on his work, and so it fell out that the pale, thoughtful Jack forgot to close the switch at Greenville one night, and put a fast freight, that was following the express, in the ditch.

For that inexcusable carelessness he was discharged, and it was not until Tommy had almost exhausted his influence at the general office that he was re-employed as flagman on a work train.

Mary, Jack's sister, had written Tommy from the convent at St. Louis, urging him to help her unfortunate brother, who seemed to be in bad repute with the officials, who apparently had forgotten that poor Jack " had risked his life " to save the Midnight Express from train robbers when a mere boy.

Tommy, remembering the sad face of the girl who had been the one close friend of his brief childhood, did what he could for her brother, but he would have done that without the letter.

Out of his savings Tommy had helped his father to build a new house at Silver Creek, and when he saw the old folks comfortably settled in it, he was contented, or as nearly so as an ambitious, aspiring youth looking for promotion can be.

Alas, for the uncertainty of railroading! Eternal vigilance, it may be said, is the price of a job. A man must so live and work, that when he leaves one road another will be waiting for him.

The Vandalia elected a new President. A new General Manager was appointed and a general cleaning out followed.

The Passenger Agent, who had taken so much interest in Tommy, retired for a time, and Tommy determined to go West and grow up with the railroads of that region.

He made a long visit at St. Jacobs, and found that his little sweetheart was dead to the world. She had taken the veil, and so shut herself away from the world that had ever seemed hard and heartless to her.

It was with a sense of pride and a shade of sadness that the agent at St. Jacobs said goodbye to his *protégé*, who boarded the Highland accommodation with a heart full of hope and a ticket for Denver.

CHAPTER XIII

MCGUIRE LEARNS TELEGRAPHY

OMAHA hung out the first flag on young McGuire as he hurried westward in the wake of the Star of Empire. Looking far into the future he saw the necessity of learning the language of the wire that had just been stretched across the plains. There were schools of telegraphy, but he chose the office, and, having shown good letters and a disposition to work, he was given employment, or rather an opportunity to learn the business.

Being accustomed to office work he soon fitted in, and made friends with all the operators, which helped him greatly. The present General Manager of the great line that at that time had just been opened to the Rocky Mountains, it is said, was one of the old employees who gave aid and encouragement to the young railroader: and the venerable President of the Gould system in the West recalls with pride that Tom McGuire was once an operator in his office at Omaha. To be sure there are many, many more who rocked the cradle of our hero, but of these above mentioned we know. The successful railway man is often amazed at the number of officials who "made him," just as the great writer is constantly crossing the trail of the man who "discovered" him.

When McGuire had mastered the key he was given a station. He was duly appointed station master, ticket agent, operator, yardmaster, head switchman, and superintendent of the windmill and water tank at Plainfield, far out on the plains.

Carefully and tenderly the superintendent of telegraph broke the news to the young man that he would have to sleep in the depot, and would, until some enterprising caterer opened a hotel, be obliged to do his own cooking. The depot had "filled" walls, the superintendent said, so there would be little danger. Upon inquiry, the young man learned that the station was built of boards, outside and inside, with four inches of sand between them.

"What's that for?" asked McGuire.

"Oh, to keep out the cold and — things.

But you must not rely wholly upon that. You must work and sleep in your six-shooters and keep your rifle in easy reach, day and night."

McGuire believed, until it was too late to back out of an ugly job, that the superintendent of telegraph was only having fun with him. .

Three days later, when the west-bound passenger train stopped at Plainfield, the new station agent stepped off. The express messenger kicked off a bundle of bedding and a few boxes of supplies, some flour and bacon, and a small cook stove.

McGuire cast one sweeping glance over Plainfield, and turning to the brakeman, asked: "Where's the station?"

For answer the brakeman gave the operator a withering look, and then putting his gloved hand upon the little board shanty that stood beside the track, said: "Johnny, you mus' be goin' bline! here's yer station, see? right here."

At that moment the train pulled out, and when the station agent had glanced up and down the track and out over the plain on either side, he realized that the brakeman had told the truth, for, if we except the windmill and the water tank, this was the only "improvement" at Plainfield.

Down the track he could see the rear end of the departing train, contracting and sinking nearer and nearer to earth. Faint and far away came the roar of wheels, and even as he looked, the last car dropped below the line of the horizon, the sound ceased, and he listened for other sounds, but there were none. He looked longingly to see some living thing, but there was neither bird nor beast in sight. He glanced along the level plain that lay cold and gray at the end of autumn, but there was not a living, moving thing upon the earth, not even a snake or horned toad. A timid man would have been helpless with fear, but young McGuire was one of those rare beings who never knew that feeling in the least. What impressed him now was the unutterable dreariness of the place. His whole being was filled with a sense of loneliness, hitherto unknown to him. Seated upon one of the boxes, he was gazing at the ground, when, to his great relief, a little brown animal with dark stripes down its back came from under the shanty, sat on the end of a tie, and looked at him. It was no larger than a small rat, but it lived and moved, and it was welcome. Now, if this thing could live in this desert alone, a man ought to exist, and the operator took heart.

Fishing a key from his pocket that had a tag upon which was written "Plainfield," he unlocked the big padlock and pushed the door open. As he did so he noticed that the door, which was also "filled," and thick like the door of a refrigerator car, was full of holes. Walking 'round the house he found that the outer walls were perforated. The holes, he reasoned, must have been made by things. He remembered that the superintendent of telegraph had said that the sand was put between the walls "to keep out the cold — and things." Coming round to the door again he went in. The place had been occupied before. There was a chair and a table and some twisted wire, but the telegraph instrument had been taken away. A small coal stove, red with rust, stood on the floor. The floor was also rusty. No, it was not rust; it was blood. So the agent, too, had been taken away. McGuire examined the walls, and noticed with a feeling of satisfaction that none of the things had penetrated the inner boards.

In a low lean-to he found fuel, and concluded to unpack and make the best of the hard lay-out, for McGuire was not a quitter. With a rusty hatchet that he had unearthed in the shed he began opening his freight. The first long box contained a rifle, two six-shooters, and many rounds of ammunition. Another held sugar and coffee, and from a third he got a neat medicine chest that contained cotton bandages and liniment. Scenting the biscuits and bacon, the little brown squirrel came nosing 'round the freight, and the agent, appreciating its company, gave it bits of cracker, and gained a companion. The first work of the operator was to examine his fire-arms and load them. He was not an expert with a rifle, but he had been three winters in St. Louis, and he reasoned that a man who could hit a snipe on the wing with a shot-gun ought to be able to hit a Sioux on his door-sill with a six-shooter.

When he had carried all his belongings into

the shanty and the shed, and had spread his bedding upon the hard board bunk, he sat down upon an empty box to think. The sun, big and red, was burning down the west at the end of a short squaw-summer day. Out of the east the shades of night came creeping across the sea of sage-brush, and the operator turned to contemplate the glory of the sunset. When the red disc was cut in half by the line of the horizon, the lone man fixed his eyes upon it and held them there. Far out on the plain, a long, lean animal, that looked to be part sheep and the rest dog, limped across the face of the falling sun, and immediately disappeared in the gloaming.

The operator entered the shanty, and in the fading light tried to connect his instrument to the broken wire that was upon the pine table. On the morrow a man would come from Kearney and fix it for him; but McGuire was lonely. If he could talk to Omaha, two or three hundred miles away, the operator there would be company for him. He worked patiently until it was dark, and then lighted his lamp. He had been so interested in the wire that he had forgotten to cook supper. He made coffee and ate some crackers and a short roll of indefinite meat. Presently he heard the roar of an approaching train. He opened the door. The rails were clicking as though they were out in a hail-storm. Now they began to sing, and a moment later the fast mail crashed by and showed her tail lights to the agent at Plainfield. It was eleven o'clock when the young operator got his instrument connected and in shape to talk to Omaha. The next moment brought answer to his call, and a great load was lifted from the young man's mind. He no longer felt lonely, for he could hear the wire talking to him, and it gave him courage. He turned to the west and called up station after station, and they all answered cheerily and gave him welcome over the wire. The operators along the line knew him for a new man, but they knew he was no coward or he would not be sleeping out in that manner. Presently, when the wire was free, they began to jolly the new agent. Kearney advised him to take off his boots when he went to bed, so as to avoid the chance of dying with them on. North Platte told him to put his hair outside the door, so the Sioux could get it without waking him. "Oh, you'll like the place," said Lincoln; "good night."

McGuire made no answer to these playful shots. The situation, from his point of view, was far from funny.

Having barred the doors and placed his firearms within easy reach, the agent at Plainfield rolled up in his blankets and tried to sleep. Far out on the desert he heard a lone wolf howl. That, thought he, is the shadow that crossed the sun.

CHAPTER XIV

STATION-MASTER MCGUIRE

THE new station-agent at Plainfield saw the sun rise on the morrow of his first night on the plains. He had watched it sinking in the sage-covered Sahara on the previous evening with a feeling of loneliness, and now he welcomed the return of day with all the enthusiasm of his youthful nature. He almost enjoyed the novelty of preparing his own breakfast, of bread, bacon, and black coffee. A long freight lumbered by, and the conductor, hanging low from the corner of the way-car, dropped off a delay report, and the operator scanned it eagerly. When the caboose had dropped from the horizon he sat down and told Omaha how a dragging brake-beam had ditched a car of ore and he was glad, for it gave him something to do and an opportunity to show his usefulness; but he did n't send that over the wire. He busied himself putting things to rights in his bachelor home, and it was noon before the day had seemed fairly begun. When the west-bound passenger train came by the express car gave up a full kit of tools to the station-master. An axe, a hammer, a saw, a pick and shovel, and a case of eggs. The Union Pacific Company was liberal with the men who helped them to open the great trail across the plains, and helped them to keep it open. McGuire watched the train, as he had watched each and every train that had come and gone since his arrival, until the rear car sank below the level of the plain. When he prepared his supper his little friend, the ground squirrel, came and sat in the door and ate crumbs. When the shadows began to creep across the plain from the east the agent sat by the door of his hut and watched the twilight deepen on the dreary plain. Between him and the glow in the west that marked the spot where the sun went down, he saw the same gaunt shadow that he had seen limping across the face of the sun on the previous evening. Still farther away he saw a horse outlined against the pink sky. Its rider sat, a bunchy, bareheaded being, that might be half man and half bear. The agent could make out that the horseman wore a blanket and feathers, and that he was gazing at the little station. McGuire had been aiming at the coyote when the Indian came up out of the west, where all things seemed to come from, if we save the sun, and now, to show the skulking Sioux that he was armed, he let go at the wolf. It was a long shot, but the boy had aimed well, having the pink sky beyond, and the wolf leaped high and fell dead, only a thousand feet from the Sioux. The Indian having marked the performance of the marksman, turned his horse's head and rode slowly away to the north. The agent knew that the Government troops had been battling with the Sioux over on Pole Creek, and made no doubt that this was a scout from the dangerous tribe. He would have reported the incident to Omaha, but he was afraid of being laughed at over the wire by the other operators along the line. Sitting there in the twilight he began to wonder what he should do if this Indian came back with a few dozen or a few hundred followers. He could bar the door and kill a few while they stormed the station, but when they had kindled a fire under the shack he must surely perish in the flames. It was not a pretty picture, and he determined to go to work at once upon a more substantial fortification. He dreaded the dreary darkness of the house, and so sat in the twilight until the gold faded from the sunset and the little brown mouse went away to bed. "God takes care of the little squirrel," mused McGuire, "and he'll take care of me as well;" and he too went to bed, but not to sleep. He lay awake planning how best to fortify the place. After dwelling upon, and then dismissing, many schemes, he decided to dig a tunnel from beneath the floor of the shed, under the railroad track and across to the water tank. If the Sioux came he could make a hard fight and then take to the tunnel and hide in the tank, for they would not be apt to burn that, having their eyes upon the burning station, watching for the agent to come out and be killed. His first plan was to dig out the tunnel without disturbing the surface of the ground, but that would take too long. He would work from the top, making a short section each day and covering the ditch over with boards and dirt as he went along, so that if any Sioux should come scouting about they might not know of the tunnel. Away off to the west he heard a wolf howl. The cry of the coyote was answered by another nearer the station, and by another and yet another still farther away. Presently he heard a low scratching on the outer shed door, and, after a long time, he fell asleep.

The sun was shining when the agent woke. The brown squirrel was sitting in the centre of the room, waiting for his breakfast.

When McGuire had made breakfast the squirrel came and ate from the agent's hand. Having finished his morning meal and reported the through freight on time, the station-master got out his pick and shovel and began his tunnel. First he made a trap door in the floor of the shed and excavated a place to drop into. Going out he measured off the distance to the tank. It was sixty feet, and he set himself the task of doing twenty feet a day and covering up the sign.

On the second morning he was stiff and lame, and his hands were so sore that he could scarcely close his fingers on the pick handle, but he worked on, and at night had the tunnel completed under the track. At the close of the third day he went into the shed, dropped to the mouth of the tunnel, crawled through, and came out in the base of the water tank that was boarded up from the ground to the tank proper. Before retiring he carried a goodly supply of cartridges and stored them in the framework of the tank near the top, and then sat down to watch the sunset. The same glory flooded the west, and when the sun was down the same gaunt shadows came and stood in the gloaming, only more of them. They had begun to scent the food supply at the station and so grew less timid. The agent had by this time determined that it was only a waste of ammunition to shoot the hungry brutes, and when he showed no fight the wolves came so near that he could have reached them with a stone. Far away he thought he heard the roar of an approaching train. The muffled sound grew louder, but looking where the two shining threads of steel drew close together, and dipped down into the desert, he could see no break on the horizon. Sweeping the plain with his eager eyes he saw a black something coming out of the north-west. It looked like a low black cloud just rising from the earth. The strange sound grew louder, and the agent thought of the sudden storms of which he had read, but the quiet sky gave no sign of storm. Already he could see a big star burning in the west. The growling cloud came nearer with each passing moment, but still lay close to the sage-brush. It grew broader but no higher, and in its wake a gray fog arose, like the mist that hangs over a swamp on a summer's morning. Higher and higher the gray cloud rose, trailing behind the black one, like the smoke from a locomotive. In a little while it covered the whole west and shut out the light from the far pink sky. The wolves, lifting their heads, listened to the roar of the advancing cloud. The darkness deepened as the roar of the cloud increased. The agent, with his rifle resting on his arm, stood and stared down the plain. A moment later the head of the cloud swept across the track just below the water tank. It looked like a regiment of cavalry riding the desert. It must be so, for he could hear hoofs rattling over the rails and crossties. Now the agent observed that they were riderless horses,— horses with horns, — and realized that this was no cloud, but a band of buffalo. He could see neither the beginning nor the end of the herd, and raising his rifle he began pumping lead into the flying band. With a great crash one of the animals drove its head against the base of the water tank and then lay still while the drove galloped past. The roar of ten thousand feet beating the desert, the wild snorts of the wounded brutes, and the mad rush of the flying mass, so excited the agent that he ran forward firing as he went into the dark and roaring flood. Presently the noise began to die down, and the agent, standing in a cloud of dust, knew that the end had come and that the dark cloud was vanishing down the desert.

When the dust had fallen McGuire found a fine calf that had driven its poor head against the tank and broken its neck. There was not a scratch upon its hide, so all his bullets had gone wide of the mark or had been carried away under the shaggy coats of the wild cattle. Here was fresh meat for the agent, but before he could remove the animal's robe the hungry wolves were pressing about in the twilight. They grew so bold that McGuire was obliged to take what he could carry and fly for the house. Before he could reach the door the wolves were snapping and fighting over the feast. Their howls and cries brought a great band, and when they had finished with what was left outside they came clawing at the shed door, demanding the agent's share. It was many hours before he could find relief from the din in unquiet dreams.

CHAPTER XV

THE COMING OF THE SIOUX

McGUIRE had been at Plainfield just a month, and had begun to believe that the place was not so dangerous after all. He was watching the sunset, and the darkness deepening upon the desert waste one evening, when he saw a speck upon the plain just where the earth met the sky. It was a shapeless bunch, too big for a wolf and too small, he thought, for a horse. As he looked it moved along the plain to the north-west and soon disappeared in the gathering gloom. The agent was still seated upon the box at the door of the depot when a big black bunch showed up just where the other smaller object had disappeared. Nearer and nearer it came, and finally stopped a few hundred yards from the station shanty. Two horsemen rode out of the black spot and approached the station. They had feathers in their hair and rifles on their arms, seeing which, the agent brought out his rifle and let it rest upon his lap. A hundred yards from the station the two men stopped and called to the agent in a strange tongue, and when he made no reply they rode slowly up to the little station. They made sign for drink, but the man stood at the door and shook his head. They would eat, but the agent refused to understand, and one of the Indians started to enter the station. The agent sprang inside, slammed the door and shoved his rifle out through the small square hole in the centre of the shutter. The Indians climbed upon their cayuses, wiggled their heels, and rode slowly back to where the band was waiting. McGuire listened at the shed door, and in a little while heard the unshod feet of the Indian ponies beating the dusty plain. They seemed to have separated, and were now galloping to surround the station. Peeping through the small port-holes the agent could see the dark line of horses closing in upon the little wooden shanty. Turning to the key he called Kearney and told them that he was being surrounded by the Sioux. Major North was notified, and started a company of scouts for Plainfield. The operator called McGuire, but got no answer, and all believed that the young station-master had been killed immediately after sending his Macedonian message. McGuire was busy. He had opened the exercises himself, firing first from one side and then from the other, to show the enemy that he was numerous and well armed. The Indians returned the fire, and the lead fairly hailed upon the house. They had charged the station, but some of the horses having been hit by the bullets fired from the stuffed walls, the Sioux fell back. They had no thought, however, of abandoning the fight, and before McGuire had succeeded in reloading his fire-arms they charged again. This time they reached the shanty, and, dismounting, beat upon the sand-filled doors in a vain effort to batter them down. The agent had been almost panic stricken at the sound of the first volley that rattled like rain upon the boarded sides of the little depot, but now all feeling of fear had left him, and he determined to give a good account of himself. Dodging from one part of the building to another he kept pouring the lead out through the narrow port-holes until the Indians were driven away again. Many were wounded, some were dead, and the rest desperate. Leaving their horses out of range of the agent's rifle, the band concentrated their efforts upon the front door. By the sound of the bullets that hailed upon the house, the agent could tell that they were coming only from one direction, and so kept his place at the side of the shanty nearest the track. He could hear them ripping boards from the framework of the water tank, and with them beating upon the heavy door. Upon the low table he had arranged boxes of cartridges and now stood in the dark room loading and emptying his revolvers. The noise of the assault upon the outer walls of the wooden building became deafening, and the horror of his surroundings almost chilled the blood of the besieged; but he had nothing to hope for at the hands of these desperate Indians, and so fought on doggedly, leaving the rest with God, the despatcher, and Major North.

Suddenly they hit the door a blow that shook the walls and the very floor of the house. They had succeeded in loosening a tie, and with it were ramming the shanty. At the same time the agent became aware of smoke in the station, and instantly started for his tunnel. They had fired the shed at the rear while assaulting the front, and the smoke almost choked McGuire as he groped his way to the opening. Through cracks in the roof he could see the fire eating its way. Already the outer wall had burned off, the sand had fallen out, and now the end of a cross-tie was driven through the ceiling, and fell, amid a shower of sparks and burning splinters, upon the floor at the agent's feet.

The front door now gave way under the heavy blows, but smoke and flames filled the place and made it impossible for the Indians to enter. As McGuire took to the tunnel he heard the yell of victory that went up from the wild band as the door fell in.

In a few moments McGuire, almost exhausted and gasping for breath, found himself in the base of the tank. When he had rested himself, he climbed to the top of the tank and, peeping from a small window, saw the painted devils prancing over the plain waiting impatiently for him to come from the burning building. In the light of the flaming station he could see them plainly, and he longed to make targets of their feathered heads, but he feared to attract their notice.

As the flames devoured the little pine house and the heat grew less intense, the bloodthirsty band peered into the ruins, and when they could see no sign of the late occupant of the place, began circling round, searching in the sage-brush for the missing man. Satan seemed to have inspired one of the imps at this moment, for, taking a brand from the ruined station, he ran and placed it against the tank. When McGuire saw what the Sioux had done he gave him a shot, and so published the secret of his hiding-place.

The moment he had fired he realized his mistake, for when once they had discovered him there would be no shadow of a show for him. Those of the Indians who had heard the shot and had seen the Sioux fall, ran about the tank looking for the agent. Presently one of the savages stopped and pointed toward the top of the tank. A great crowd had now collected, and when they had jabbered about the dead Indian, the tank, and the telegrapher for a few moments they threw up their guns and sent a shower of shot against the wooden structure. The agent, crouching close to the water tub, kept out of the way and held his fire. Presently he heard them batter the door down. A moment later he knew that they were climbing up the narrow ladder. He waited at the top, and when the first feathered head showed above the landing at the bottom of the tank proper he brought the barrel of his rifle down and the Sioux fell upon the one following him, knocking him from the ladder, and so they all went tumbling to the ground. Leaning from his hiding-place, McGuire emptied a six-shooter into the confused band, and they were glad enough to escape, dragging their dead and wounded with them. Being sure of the whereabouts of the white man, the Indians determined to have him out at any cost. While the major part of the band trained their guns upon the tank, a half-dozen Indians carried fire-brands and heaped them up against the framework. The splinters of the broken door were used for kindling, and soon the flames were running up the side of the tank, lighting up the plain for five hundred yards around.

With a sinking heart McGuire saw the semicircle of light from his funeral-pyre drive the darkness from the desert, and knew that in a little while he must choose between this burning refuge and the blood-thirsty band below. The fight, of which he had been so full a few moments ago, had all gone out of him, and for the first time in his life he lost heart. He was so appalled at the thought of the awful death that awaited him that it became a labor to breathe. His limbs grew leaden. His rifle was so heavy that he laid it down, and, leaning over the top of the tank, ran his fingers through his hair and was surprised that it was tangled and wet, like fine grass heavy with dew. Clasping his empty hands he lifted his eyes to heaven to ask for help, but his glance was arrested at the horizon where a big star burned above the plain. As he looked the star grew brighter, and he was reminded of the story of a world that had been as hopelessly lost as he seemed now, when a star burned in the east and the world was saved. Suddenly behind the star a yellow light flared, fan-shaped, from the earth, and he knew that the star was the headlight of a locomotive and the flash was from the furnace where the fireman was shovelling coal for dear life. Now the rails that were glistening in the glare of the headlight and bridging the darkness to the edge of the light of the burning tank began to sing, and the Indians took warning and fled into the darkness.

"Too late, too late!" said the captain of the scouts, who was riding in the cab.

The engineer made no reply, but tugged at the throttle, that was already wide open, and kept his eyes fixed upon the burning building. "That will do," he said to the fireman as the light of his head-lamp reached the other light. He made a motion with his left hand as of a man drinking, and the fireman put on the lefthand pump to save the boiler, for the water was low in the lower gauge.

"Too late, too late!" mused McGuire, as the flames climbed to the top and a red tongue lipped the edge of the tank as a mad dog laps a running brook. Until now he had not thought of trying to escape, for only death had waited at the bottom, but seeing the Sioux hunting cover, he peered over the edge, and the smoke and flames were all about the ladder. Now the fire burst through and the smoke came up blinding and hot, and he took a last stand on the narrow bridge that ran over the top of the water tub. As he climbed up his hands touched the water in the tank, which till now he had not thought of. The tank was level full, and with his hands he began to scoop the water out, and in a little while succeeded in checking the fire that was eating round to the rear; but it was too far advanced in front, next to the track, to be put out so easily. With a great effort he managed to reach the rope that was fixed to the valve in the bottom of the tank, and when he had opened it the great volume of water rushed out and deadened the fire, so that by staying in the bottom of the empty tank McGuire was able to survive until the captain of the scouts and a couple of Pawnees reached the top of the charred structure and carried him, almost lifeless, into the fresh open air.

"Little emergency runs like that," said the superintendent to the engineer afterwards, "make men appreciate the value of time."

CHAPTER XVI

McGUIRE GOES SWITCHING

PUEBLO was a tough town when the Rio Grande terminated at that point. All the good men were going into the mountains, for Leadville was then sweating silver that was worth more than a dollar an ounce. To be sure there were always a few reliable men who could railroad, who knew nothing else, and would do nothing else. There were Dan Snyder, Steve Riley, Jud Rogers, Charlie Barnes, and Silversmith, old timers and stayers, whose signals were always safe, and upon these men the management depended to handle the trains and hold the "stormy" switchmen in line. It was at this swift outpost on the edge of the west that Tom McGuire tied up and asked Jim Williams, the "scrappy" yardmaster, for a job, switching in the yards.

"Where ye frum?" asked Suicide Dick, the foreman, cocking his cigar in one corner of his mouth and then blowing rings of smoke into the twilight, as he strolled down the yard with the new man.

"The U. P."

"Umaha?"

"Yes."

"Know Pat Toohey?"

"No."

"Then yer a liar, Mr. McGuire, ye never saw Umaha — gimme that glim."

Now, McGuire had never been called a liar. He was not a liar, and he knew it, but he gave the foreman the glim, just over the left eye.

"You dam farmer," said Dick, and that was all he said. He put down his white light and put up his hands.

McGuire saw that he was about to have a fight with a man whom he had known less than ten minutes. He made his feet firm on the coarse gravel and waited. Dick wiped his bleeding eye on his jumper sleeve and looked for an opening. McGuire put up his hands awkwardly.

Dick smiled.

Scrappy Jim saw the men manœuvring in the twilight and signalled a switch-engine back with a rush signal, whirling his lamp furiously until the pony had stopped in front of the switch-shanty.

"Smatter?" demanded fighting John Jones, leaning from the cab. He did not like the signal. It seemed to him that it carried an unnecessary amount of "hurry up." Without lifting his eyes to the cab, Jim stepped aboard, and, nodding down the yard, said, "Back up. Suicide's touchin' up the new guy."

Jones opened the throttle and the yard engine slid down the track and stopped short where the trouble was. Dick heard the engine and was glad. He liked an audience. He remembered how the yardmaster had " touched him up " in the first hour of his first day's work for the company, and recalled with pride that the good showing he had made with Jim had won promotion. McGuire had expected that the yardmaster on the engine and the engineer would stop the fight, but he heard no word from them. Only three suns had set since this pugilistic pair had shut themselves up in a box car and settled their own little differences, and they now leaned side by side from the cab window and looked with much interest upon the argument that was about to take place.

"Here they come," said Dick, playfully, and he reached for McGuire's face.

"We ride everything here. Here comes a flat fur a starter," and he spanked McGuire's cheek with his open hand. "Here's an empty box," and he reached for the other side, but McGuire's arm was on his time.

"That's right — stop 'em. Here's a cripple for the rep track," and he landed lightly on McGuire's ribs. "Here's a couple loaded," and he put his right and left hard on McGuire's chest.

The blows angered the tenderfoot. Dick was leaping and dancing about the unfortunate stranger as a savage Sioux would leap about a scalped Pawnee. "We'll put this express car in on the spur," said Dick as he landed a stinging blow on the point of his opponent's nose. That insult brought the blood, and instantly all the Irish in McGuire's make-up came to the surface. He was desperate, but he knew he must keep cool. The foreman began to force the fighting. He talked less now, but fought more. McGuire contented himself with stopping the blows of his adversary, and so saved his wind, which he had observed was a tender point in this rare, light air. Dick was wearing himself out. His left eye was bleeding and the blood blinded him at times. McGuire would not wilfully take advantage of that, but the yardman kept him so busy and mixed cuts for him to such an extent, that he had to do something.

"Here's a gondola loaded with iron ore," said Dick, and he made a curve with his left, which McGuire dodged. Before the foreman could recover, McGuire swung his right on the fellow's left ear, and Suicide Dick collapsed like a punctured tire.

"That must 'a been a sleeper," said Jim, glancing at Jones.

McGuire stood puffing like a helper on a heavy grade, and waiting for Dick to get to his feet.

The two men came from the engine and stood by the man on the ground.

Dick lifted his head and then sat up. Presently he got to his feet, and when he could see, he picked out McGuire and offered his hand. McGuire took it, and then Jones offered his hand, and then the yardmaster shook the hand of the tenderfoot.

Dick walked over to a freight engine, opened the water-cock, and bathed his bleeding face.

"Wash up," said Williams, jerking his thumb in the direction of the freighter, and McGuire went over and washed.

"I want to pay for that light before I go," said McGuire, "and I owe this man an apology for striking him with it."

"Huh," grunted Dick.

"Don't git silly," said Jim.

Dick handed his lamp, which had a frosted stripe near the top of the globe, to McGuire, and picked up the bent and battered frame that awhile ago had fallen across his face.

"Don't I quit?" asked McGuire, glancing from one face to the other.

"Quit! what do you quit fur? Did n't you win? They don't nobody quit — you simply change places; an' when you lick me you 'll be yardmaster, an' have two stripes on yer glim, see?"

McGuire could not reply. He was utterly unable to make these men out, and when Jones had climbed on to the engine, he stepped with the yardmaster on to the footboard, Dick, who was tired, took a seat on the bumper beam between them, and the little switcher trembled away down the track to where a freight conductor was swearing loudly in front of the switch-shanty.

When the road had been extended to Leadville young McGuire, having attracted the notice and won the respect of the Superintendent, was sent up to take charge of the yards. Switchmen were scarcer there than they had been at Pueblo, for the town was wild and wide open. Those who came to work in the yards were the toughest of the tough, men who could not find employment east of Denver came here to railroad, ten thousand feet above the sea. McGuire undertook to improve the service. He put up a bulletin that said men must not fight on duty, and that all switchmen would be expected to be sober when they reported for work; that trainmen would be allowed but one place of residence, and that the caller would not look further than the address given for men who were wanted.

"All switchmen," said Flat-wheel Finigan, from the Texas Pacific, reading the bulletin. "Now, it's plain to me that that 'all' means 'Finigan,'" and the new bulletin was ripped ruthlessly from the wall of the yard-house.

If McGuire discharged a man, a worse one came to fill the vacancy; and the yardmaster became discouraged. He sent in his resignation, but no attention was paid to it. Nobody came to relieve him, and so he worked on, always short-handed and often alone. Winter came, and it was next to impossible to get men to handle the company's business. A large force of laborers was kept constantly at work shovelling snow from the many spurs that ran up to the mines or down to the smelters. Of course McGuire could only offer schedule pay that was fixed at Denver, and it was hard to get men to switch in the snow for three dollars when they could have five for sawing wood or tending bar.

After much correspondence the yardmaster succeeded in having the pay of switchmen raised to four dollars in the Leadville yards, and in a little while had a reasonably sober gang chasing the three yard engines that had been sent up to do the work of four.

Things went fairly well until the foreman got drunk one day, and had to be discharged. The wronged man went over to the Cadillac and told his troubles to the barkeeper. His tale was overheard by a lucky miner who had just sold a prospect hole for ten thousand. This miner, with the liberality of a man moved by spirits, proposed that the two open a saloon-restaurant. He would furnish the money, the yardman the experience, nerve, and good-will. The offer was accepted. They bought a storeroom that had cost six hundred for sixteen, and in less than a week from the day of his dismissal the ex-foreman posted the following notice above his front door: —

"Wanted — Seven swift biscuit shooters, any sex, creed, or color — Wages, six dollars a day."

Thirty minutes later seven of McGuire's switchmen were switching in the "Green Café."

Later one of the men went back and brought the foreman from the yards, who was installed as yardmaster in the new restaurant. The manager became the "G. M.," and the talk was railroad talk and nothing else.

The "switch-list" was not printed, but was shown orally to each patron as he took his seat.

"Ride 'em in, ride 'em in," called the yardmaster to a couple of switchmen who were pitching plates of beans through a narrow window from the kitchen to the dining-room.

"Drop the dope down the main line;" and one of the men shot a yellow bowl of butter on to the centre table.

"Sand on No. 1 — north spur," called the head waiter, and before he had finished a sugar-bowl was dropped upon the first table to the right.

"Pull the pin on that load on No. 2 south," yelled the general manager. The yardmaster and one of the switchmen lifted a fat man from the sawdust floor and put him in a back room to cool.

"Pancakes, warm, please," said a man who seemed to be afraid of being overheard.

"String o' flats with a hot box," called the yardmaster; and so it went from morning till midnight, and from midnight till morning again.

In the mean time McGuire worked loyally for the company, freezing his ears and frosting his feet. One bitter cold morning a string of empties got away on the hill. All the switchmen, who were not switchmen at all, but who were drawing pay under false pretensions, jumped off in the deep snow. McGuire stayed with the train and rode them down. The agent at Malta saw them coming round the curve up toward the town, and saw McGuire signalling frantically for the safety switch, — a short spur that was put there to keep runaway cars from getting out on the main line on the time of regular trains. That was a trying moment for the station-agent. If he threw McGuire in on the spur he would be shot down the hill with a half-dozen freight cars on top of him. If he let him out on to the main line, he must almost surely collide with the up-coming passenger train that had already passed Haydens and could not be caught by wire. He knew McGuire and liked him. He was awed by the great courage that could hold a single man on

a runaway train on such a hill at such a time.
There was something fine in the make-up of a
man who could call for a switch to wreck himself to save the crew and passengers on another
train. The agent signalled the yardmaster to
get off, but McGuire shook his head. The
agent turned his back, and McGuire went out
on the main line, leaning to the curve like a
man driving a fast horse on a circular course.
Below the station there was a short stretch of
straight track from which the wind, blowing
down from Tennessee Pass, had swept the
snow. The yardmaster, climbing from car to
car, set the brakes as tight as he could set them;
but the shoes were covered with ice, and the
train, on the tangent, seemed to be increasing
its speed. Now they fell into a lot of curves.
McGuire began to guess that he could not hold
them; but he could not get off now, even if he
chose to do so, for on one hand lay the Arkansas River and on the other the rock wall of the
cañon.

Far down the gulch he heard a locomotive
whistle, and his heart stood still. Presently he
felt the brakes taking hold of the wheels. It

seemed incredible, but it was so. The friction of the whirling wheels had melted the ice from the brake shoes, and now the wheels began to smoke. The curves and reverse curves helped also, and the runaway train began to slow down. He could easily jump now, if they failed to stop, for they were not making twenty miles an hour; but at that moment he heard a wild, distressing cry for brakes from a locomotive. He was riding on the rearmost car, the head end was hidden round a sharp curve, and now he saw the middle of his train hump up like a cat's back. The first car shot up over the pilot of the head engine, cut off her stack, whistle, and one corner of her cab, but fortunately no one was hurt.

That afternoon McGuire promoted the foreman to be yardmaster, went to Denver and resigned "in person;" but his resignation was not accepted.

CHAPTER XVII

SNOWBOUND

DOWN on the desert the earth was warm and brown, but when the train had passed Grand Junction a few stray flakes were seen floating across the cañon. At Montrose, where they picked up a helper for the hill, the ground was covered with snow. Most of the passengers got out and walked up and down the long wooden platform, for the air was cool and bracing. It seemed that there must be some trouble up the line, for the conductor of No. 8 was hurrying to and fro with his hands full of orders that he appeared unable to fill. A couple of travelling men were threatening to sue the company unless they reached Denver within the next twenty-four hours; and other passengers were getting hungry. Jack Bowen, of the Ouray branch, was lying luminously to a dignified New Englander and his handsome daughter. Jack was the uniformed conductor of the Ouray run, whose elocutionary accomplishments had made him the envy of all the men on the mountain division of this mountainous railroad. They had ploughed up a tribe of Indians coming down that morning, Jack was saying, with his insinuating, half-embarrassed smile, and the pilot of the locomotive had been red with the blood of the band.

"Look now, you can see the fireman cleaning it off," he added, for the old gentleman was going to smile. Sure enough they could see the fireman with a piece of waste wiping the pilot of the Ouray engine.

"And did you leave them where they lay?"

"Sure," said Jack; "could n't stop the most important run on the road for a few miserable Ingins, — dead Ingins at that. 'Sides, if we stopped we could n't get 'em."

"Was the snow so very deep up there?"

"'T want the snow," said the conductor, smiling and consulting his big gold watch.

"What was it, then?" asked the tourist, becoming more and more interested.

"Well, it so happened that a band of wolves was at that moment passin' down towards the

Uncompahgre in search of food, an' the moment they got scent o' blood they pounced upon the prey."

The young lady caught her father's arm and shuddered.

"If there is anything a wolf rolls as a sweet morsel under his tongue," said Jack, glancing at his watch again, "it's Ingin fricassee, rare and red."

"Oh, papa!" said the young lady, "let's go back to the sleeper."

"You see," resumed the conductor, "it did n't matter much, for this was a band of renegades — bad Ingins they are called, — who ought to have been killed some time ago. Their leader, Cut-Your-Hair-Short, was spotted by old Ouray, the chief, anyway. He wanted to marry Cat-A-Sleepin', Ouray's daughter; the old man kicked, and what you 'spose this Ingin, Cut-Your-Hair-Short, did?"

"I have n't the remotest idea," said the bewildered New Englander.

"Well, sir, he goes up to the old chief's hogan —"

"Bowen."

"Excuse me," said Jack, "till I explain the orders to this young man. Yo' see he's new at the business, and I have to help him out occasionally to see —"

"Bowen."

This time the conductor of No. 8 spoke short and sharp, and Bowen went to him.

"Now, look here, Jack," began the conductor of the snow-bound train, "if you don't stop stuffing that old gentleman I swear I'll report you when I get to Salida."

"Who's stuffin' 'im?"

"That's all right, you lie to your own people — let my passengers alone."

Jack went back to his prey.

"I hope," said the gray-haired voyager, "that this young man will not get us into any trouble."

"Oh! not a bit of it, not a bit of it; I have explained everything to him, and he won't forget. Now, you'd never dream it," he went on, turning and walking beside the handsome woman, "but that young fellow McGuire's a nobleman."

"You don't tell me?"

"Yes, I do, an' what's more to the point, it's true. Look at him. You don't suppose a young fellow like that would be in charge of a main line express train 'less he had a pull."

"A what?"

"'Less he cut ice elsewhere," said the conductor. "I tell you that comedian stands to win out a throne some day. His father was Irish, of course, but his mother was French. She could chase herself right back to the old rock and rye family, the Bourbins, I think they were called. His grandfather lived with a man called Louie Sais on a ranch called Ver Sigh, a little way out of Paris. The old man was a sort of a chum of the Louis, called 'The Gentleman of the Sleeping Car' or something like that, — he was a big hole at Ver Sigh, was this boy's Grand Pare."

"Allabo a-r-d," said McGuire in the middle of his career. The old gentleman bowed stiffly to Bowen, the young lady smiled sweetly, and stepped into the Pullman.

When McGuire came through the car taking up tickets after leaving Montrose, he found Miss Landon alone. She lifted her eyes, — sunny eyes, they were, that seemed to mock him and the blinding storm through which they were now rolling away up the long, even grade that made a mighty approach to the mountain. She held her glance upon his burning face for the briefest space, but when he passed on he could still feel the warmth of her eyes, like the waves of lingering sunshine through which you pass when you are walking in a summer twilight.

When he had finished his work the conductor returned to the smoking-room of the sleeper, but found after a moment's stay that the air was vile, the place stuffy, and he went forward to the day coach. As he passed through the forward sleeper he noticed that Miss Landon was still alone. She had her back to him, but as he came up the aisle the swing of the car on a short curve caused him to steady himself upon the end of her section. At the same moment and for the same reason she put an ungloved hand out to clasp the edge of the narrow seat, and it fell, soft as a snowflake, warm as a sunbeam, and soundless as a shadow, upon the hand of McGuire.

To be sure she did not leave it there long,

but she had to press the hand of the conductor to steady herself in the car that was now rolling like a stage-coach on the Rainbow Route. She drew her hand away, and went red to the tips of her shell-like ears; but she did not look back to see whose hand she had caressed. Looking into the narrow mirror at her side, McGuire saw her confusion and hurried past, and she wondered whether it was his hand that she had touched. She rather hoped that it might be so!

Up in the forward car the two travelling men, the editor of the Ouray Solid Muldoon, and a cowboy from the Uncompahgre, were playing poker. Now McGuire knew that this was against the rules of the road, but he was slow to make protest under the circumstances. He was reasonably sure that they would all come back to Montrose, for the snow was growing deeper and deeper with each passing mile-post. He would have these men on his hands overnight, and so would avoid friction. He stood with his back to the door for a moment listening to the talk of the travelling men, the cowboy, and the editor.

"Why, I know 'im like a book," Muldoon was saying. "Name's Landon, Ole Joe Landon of Gloucester, made his money on codfish: ante up there, Patsy."

"It's his do," said Patsy.

"Come to the centre there, ole brandin' iron," said the editor to the cattleman, and the latter dropped a cartridge among the coin and other equivalent upon the impoverished poker table.

Time had been when McGuire could linger and laugh for hours where these rollicking voyagers played and told stories, but now their talk seemed absolutely silly, not to say vulgar, and he turned away.

"After all," mused McGuire, "there's not such a gulf between us. She's a rich merchant's daughter, I'm a poor conductor. She must ever remain a merchant's daughter with no show for promotion. I'm due to be a superintendent, a general manager, and, possibly, the president of a railroad. And then — if she is still a merchant's daughter! well, it's a long, long road, but by the god o' the wind, I'll make the effort. If I fail, very well, I shall be better for having tried."

Seating himself in a quiet corner, McGuire began to count upon the fingers of his left hand the men who had begun far below where he now stood and worked up to positions of trust. First he counted presidents only. There were Manvill, Moffett, Newell, Blackstone, Clark of the U. P., Clark of the M. & O., Towne, Hughitt, and Van Horne. When he began on the general managers he had to go to the other hand, and when he came to count the self-made superintendents, beginning loyally with "the old man" of the mountain division, he ran out of fingers and took heart. And what a prize to work for, and she was rich. Incidentally she was an angel.

He could not tell why he did so, but he now went back through the car, and as he was passing the old merchant's section the head engine, which was wearing a pilot plough, screamed for brakes, and the train came to a dead stop.

"Anything wrong?" asked the traveller.

"Oh! no," said McGuire cheerfully, "just a little skiff o' snow."

Now, he had made up his mind not to look into the eyes of the girl again, but when she leaned over and asked, with just the sweetest, distressing little scare in her voice, if there were any wolves about, he had to look.

"No," he said, "there are no wolves in these mountains to speak of," and he smiled a smile that was almost sad.

"Nor Indians?" said the sweet voice, a trifle clearer.

"Nor Indians," said McGuire, shaking his head.

"They're dreadful on the Ouray branch."

"Which, the wolves or the Indians?"

"Both," she replied. "A gentleman told us, there where we stopped so long, that they killed ever so many Indians coming down this morning. Mr. Bowen, I think they called him; he seemed to be one of the officials of the road, so I'm sure he would not say anything to frighten people if it were not true."

McGuire was boiling. He might have been tempted to introduce Mr. Bowen then and there, but at that moment the head brakeman came back to say that they were stuck fast in a drift a hundred yards from the little telegraph office at the foot of Cerro Hill.

For nearly an hour they bucked and backed and bucked again, but it was of no use. The snow was growing deeper with each passing moment. Presently it stopped snowing and began to blow, and McGuire asked for orders to back down to Montrose again, but the despatcher would not let him go.

Denver was hammering Salida, Salida was swearing at Gunnison, and Gunnison was burning the company wire over Cerro Hill, telling McGuire to get out.

Finally the trainmaster lost his head, McGuire lost his temper, wrote his resignation and handed it to the operator, but fortunately the wires were down by this time, and the message could n't go.

The section gang having cleared the siding, the train was now pulled in off the main line.

Being assured that there were no wolves nor Indians on the right of way, Miss Landon came out with her father to see the sights. It was growing dark at the end of a short December day, and what with the flying snow and the screams and snorts of the engines that had been uncoupled and were now hammering away at the deep drifts, the merchant and his daughter were unable to hear the whistle of a snow-plough that was at that moment falling down from Cerro summit.

McGuire heard the whistle, backed his buckers on to the siding, and, looking up, saw Miss Landon and her father standing on the edge of a thorough cut that had drifted almost full of snow. Appreciating at a glance the danger they were in, the conductor ran up the track and tried to call to the old gentleman to stand back, but the snow was deep and held him, the storm muffled his voice, and the wind carried his cry away across the hills and lost it among the shrouded cedars.

The big engine, and the snow-plough, under the snow, made little more noise than a ship would make running under water, and it was not until the plough was upon them that the two travellers at the top of the cut saw or heard it. The great machine, which was rounding a slight curve, seemed to be driving straight for them. The girl turned to try to escape, and there before her, not two cars away, she saw what seemed to be a huge black bear, climbing up the bank toward her. At that moment she stepped over the edge, and went rolling down to the bottom of the cut, for the newly drifted snow was soft and light.

It would have been a relief to Miss Landon to have been able to faint, but she did not. She had no sooner reached the outer rail than the big plough picked her up and hurled her, unhurt, almost out of the right of way. She grew dizzy with the sensation of falling, but was able to feel that she was coming down on the soft snow, and that she was still unhurt. Between her going up and coming down she managed to breathe a grateful prayer, so rapidly does the human mind work at the edge of the future.

After what appeared to her a very long time, she came down in a deep drift with her eyes full of snow. She felt soft arms about her waist, and opened her eyes. "Help! help!" she screamed, for the arms were the arms of the big black bear. Now the bear stood up and carried her away. She fainted.

When the sun went down the wind went with it. The moon came up from beyond Ouray and showed the still, cold world sleeping in her robe of white. The smooth, high mountains, twenty, fifty, and even a hundred miles away, looked like polished piles of marble, gleaming in the moonlight. Miss Landon was lying on a couch in the drawing-room of a sleeper. Her father was seated opposite her, and when the conductor looked in to see if anything was wanted, the merchant asked him to sit down. The excitement through which he had passed made the old gentleman feel lonely, away out there in the wilds of a trackless waste. Possibly the stories that Bowen had told him added to his uneasiness. He wanted to smoke. All the other ladies, not having staterooms, had gone to the hotel for the night. Miss Landon was nervous and he did not like her to be alone, so now, making excuse, he went to the smoking-room.

The Ouray train had been unable to reach its destination and had also backed down to Montrose again. McGuire had given Bowen orders to keep out of his train, and Jack was hurt. He had secured a guitar, a man who could play it, some railway employees who thought they could sing, and just as the old gentleman was entering the smoking-room, Jack and his mirth-makers paused beneath Miss Landon's window. Jack had instructed them to sing "Patsy Git Up From the Fire," and to begin with the chorus.

The heart of the handsome conductor beat wildly when he found himself alone with the charming girl. Her cheeks were slightly flushed, for the excitement of the afternoon had left her feverish. Her deep blue eyes shed a softer light as she lounged upon the little divan amid the Pullman pillows.

Realizing that her duty was now that of hostess in her own drawing-room, Miss Landon was about to break the embarrassing silence that was filling the place, but at that moment Camdel, the red-haired soprano, touched the guitar and opened up with a mirth-provoking Irish accent: —

> "Arrah, Patsy! git up f'om th' fire,
>   An' guv th' mon a sate;
> Can't ye see that it 's Misther McGuire,
>   Come a courtin' yer sisther Kate?"

By the time the singers had concluded the chorus McGuire was on his feet, his face changing from red to white.

"Sit down," said Miss Landon, blushing, but smiling in spite of herself. "I did not know you had a bard among you capable of making songs upon occasion," she added; "please don't disturb them."

McGuire threw himself upon the seat and bit his lip. If only he could get hold of Jack Bowen he'd break his long back.

After what seemed an age to McGuire the song ceased.

"I think that is perfectly wonderful," said Miss Landon enthusiastically, "and how nicely the singing sounds out there in the clear, cold night. They must have made that song since we came back from the hills; and the music, where did they get the tune? Did that funny Mr. Bowen make that too?"

"That man couldn't make a mud pie; he can't whistle a tune; he can't even tell the truth," said the conductor of No. 8, indignantly.

"Oh, Mr. McGuire," said the young lady, with a pretty show of surprise.

"Well, it's true. I'm ashamed to say so, but it's true; you must not believe a word he says."

"Not one word?"

"Never. I don't see how he made his wife believe he loved her."

"Is he married, then?"

"Oh, yes. He's as gentle as a nun and as harmless as a child, only don't believe him. He lies just for the love of it, and never to injure any one. He ought to leave the road and devote himself to literature; he likes romancing. He calls his harmless bits of fiction 'Novels Out of Print.'"

"He certainly has a ready and vivid imagination."

Miss Landon sighed lightly. McGuire was handsome, and he had held her in his arms.

"Please take off that horrid woolly coat," said Miss Landon, with a little shudder.

McGuire, blushing, removed his bearskin overcoat that he had put on up in the hills that afternoon.

"I presume papa has thanked you for rescuing me so heroically," she said, looking at him.

"He has, but it was not necessary."

"But it is right, and I must thank you also."

"Then, if you thank me, I am glad, for you

did not seem to appreciate my efforts at the moment."

"Who could? I was scared out of my wits; I took you for a horrid bear, and that was the first time I ever fainted in all my life; and that's more than some of your Western girls can say, who are so sensible, self-possessed, and brave."

"I thought," said McGuire, smiling back at the young lady, "it might be because we had not been properly introduced. You have doubtless heard of the Boston girl who was drowning, but refused to be rescued upon that ground?"

"I have not heard it, and I should not believe it if I had. Boston girls are as sensible as Denver girls or San Francisco girls. I don't know that we have been introduced yet," she added, with a little toss of her head, and her words went straight to the heart of McGuire.

He felt that he ought to go, and yet he knew that her father had left her in his care, and that he would be expected to remain in the drawing-room until the merchant had finished his cigar. To add to his confusion she let her window shade fly up, and, apparently ignoring his presence, was looking out upon the cold, shrouded world, that seemed so wild and wide.

"Ah!" said the old gentleman, entering the room, "I feel better now; first good smoke I've had since dinner."

When McGuire arose and took up his greatcoat, Miss Landon stood up and returned his good night.

"Good night," said the merchant, and immediately, as if they had been waiting for time, the mirth-makers upon the platform sang:

"Good night, ladies, good night, ladies,
Sweet dreams, ladies — we're going to leave you now."

CHAPTER XVIII

BREAKING THE TRAIL

AT midnight orders came. The road was open, the wires up, and the delayed train, in three sections, pulled out for the hills. The big pilot plough that had "bucked" the beautiful Miss Landon out of the right-of-way and into the arms of McGuire ran ahead, followed by the Rockaway with two cars, while a couple of heavy mountain-climbers brought up the coaches and sleepers.

McGuire watched, like a faithful slave, at the door of the merchant's stateroom, for he was hard hit by the hand and eyes of the merchant's daughter. The heavy car rocked gently on the curves as the big engines, with much slipping and sanding, toiled to the summit of Cerro Hill. In a little while they were rolling along the banks of the Gunnison, and the silent river was slipping past them under the snow. At sunrise, having toiled up another long, hard hill, the train stood at the crest of the continent, ten thousand feet above the sea.

McGuire regretted that the old gentleman had taken a drawing-room, for when they had a section in the body of the car. the conductor could see the beautiful woman as he passed up and down. Now, if she chose to do so, she could isolate herself utterly. While the grim drivers were oiling round, the young lady appeared upon the platform, smiled at McGuire, and asked him to help her down.

"Papa's still sleeping, and I don't want to miss the view."

The conductor opened a narrow door in the big, smoky snow-shed, and they stepped out into the crisp, sunny air.

"Oh! how perfectly beautiful," exclaimed the enthusiastic girl, gazing over the top of aspen groves, where the trees were hung with millions of jewels that sparkled and quivered in the morning sun.

When the train had begun to wind away down the mountain side the conductor brought a camp-stool, and the young lady sat upon the rear platform of the rearmost car and watched the mountains spring up in their wake. Once, when they were rounding a long curve, the conductor asked her to look over the low range, Poncho Pass, that walls the San Luis away from the Arkansas Valley, and there she saw an even hundred miles of the snowy Sangre de Cristo, lifting her white crest far up into the burnished blue.

Presently, when they had dropped into the cañon, and there were no more mountains to be seen, Miss Landon asked the conductor to send her the words of the song his friends had sung to them over beyond the Rockies.

"I'll write you the chorus now, on a leaf from my train-book."

"Oh, do you remember it?"

"I ought to; I have heard it all my life."

"Then it was not made for us — for you, I mean?"

"I'm afraid not."

"Then how did it happen to have our — your name?"

"Oh, McGuire is a common Irish name, you know. But was it your name, as well? Is your name Kate?"

She smiled and nodded.

"Then my friends were innocent, for I'm sure they did not know it, or they never would have sung that song. It must have seemed awfully rude to you."

"On the contrary, I thought it extremely clever, and flattered myself that I had been the inspiration, or part of it, at least. Anyway, you'll send me the song, won't you?"

"With pleasure," and he wrote her name and waited for the address.

"Just Gloucester — everybody knows us — or papa, at least."

"Thank you," said the conductor, closing his book.

"Thank *you*."

"For what?"

"For saving the life of a poor girl and bringing her back to her papa, like a good bear, when you might have carried her away to the hills."

Now, the light engines that had helped them up the mountain began whistling for Salida.

"I get off here," said McGuire, rising.

"Oh! is this the end?"

"Of my run, yes, and this has been the best trip I ever had."

"Do you call it a good trip when you are a day late?"

"I call this a good trip. And that reminds me that I have not made out my report."

"What will you report?"

"The cause of the delay."

"And the effect?"

"Yes," said McGuire, with his heart hitting his vest like a trip-hammer, "but not now. I'll make that report when other men are reporting to me."

"I don't understand you."

"You will when you see my report. Listen! When I am the Superintendent and have outgrown this beastly uniform, I'll send you that song, and if you get it, then I'll forward my report."

He was so handsome, his eyes glowing with the light of love, his voice so full of emotion, that a woman with cooler blood than that which flowed in the veins of the Gloucester girl might have been moved.

She held out her hand (she had removed one

of her gloves) and McGuire seized it. Glancing through the glass door, he raised it to his lips, and she suffered him to do so.

She felt the ring on his finger, and remembered that she had felt it once before. It was his hand that she had pressed, accidentally, over there in the storm.

When the train swung 'round the curve and stopped at the station, the conductor touched his cap and dropped off.

When he had registered "in" he came out, and the Gloucester girl, watching at the window, saw him cross the little swinging bridge and lose himself in the narrow, unpaved streets of what, to her, seemed a dreary little town.

CHAPTER XIX

A NEW LINE

WHEN a man sets his heart on a thing he can accomplish a great deal in a comparatively short time. Thomas McGuire had been a careful, industrious employee. He had never acquired the habit of wasting all of his leisure hours and spare dollars in the wild resorts of the thriving towns that lay at either end of his run. He began now to study the history of American railways. He devoured everything in print, from the local weekly paper to the monthly magazines and reviews. He bought, begged, and borrowed books that would give him more or less of the financial history of the various railways of the country. He had the advantage of a fair education, which enabled him to read rapidly and understandingly. What he longed for and worked for was promotion, but it seemed to go by the other way. He grew impatient. To be sure, nobody ran around him, but promotion came slowly. Nobody seemed to want to quit, or get killed, and so, when the Intermountain Air Line was built, McGuire got in on the ground floor. He had the first passenger train on the road, and in a little while was made trainmaster, but there he hung for a whole year. Another step would put him in a place where he could send his song to Gloucester, but he was powerless to help himself on. At last an Assistant Superintendent was appointed and McGuire got the job.

Another man might have strained a point here and knocked, at once, at the gate of the handsome woman's walled-up heart, but McGuire was severely exact. He must not be the Assistant Superintendent, but the whole thing, and so he worked and waited until another year had gone by. Of course, promotion was bound to come to a man who worked as he worked, he knew that, and it did come one spring morning when it was least expected. He was asked to take the place of General Superintendent of a competing line. As might have been expected, one of the first things he did was to mail a copy of a certain homely song to Gloucester, as a signal of his success, and then he went to work with a will. In less than six months he had made a name for himself, crippled the Air Line, which means success in this country where competition is the life (or death) of railroading, and they asked him to come back, and proposed to double his salary. But he would not go as assistant to a man who was notoriously incompetent, and whose only excuse for being in the business was that his father had inherited money and put it into the building of the new line. It happened, however, as it frequently does, that other people had put money into the same enterprise; they were losing it, and they objected to assessments where they had expected dividends. The young man resigned; McGuire took his place, and in ninety days had pulled the business back that he had pulled away with him. When a merchant is going to ship a few cars of goods over somebody's railroad, he says to McGuire, who happens to be his personal friend, "You can do this as cheaply as the other fellows?" "Yes," says McGuire, "the rate is about the same on all lines." So it comes down to a matter of personal popularity, and McGuire gets the freight, and that's all there is to railroading, so far as getting business goes. When it comes to handling men and keeping up track, that requires a genius with colder blood.

In a little while McGuire was made General Manager, but he was unhappy. What was the good of all this success? The manuscript of the song had come back to him from the dead-letter office. He was famous in railway circles but miserable in mind. It was impossible to pick up a newspaper that ran " Railroads " without reading of the Inter-Mountain Air Line and its brilliant young manager. He was dignified enough to command the respect, and simple and democratic enough to win the love, of his subordinates. He looked to the heads of the various departments to manage the business, but watched over it all himself. He was always accessible. He could awe a manager's meeting or he could put in a frog.

He never locked his door.

CHAPTER XX

COMING HOME

> She gazed on the old things of Egypt and India,
> Sighed o'er the ruins of Athens and Rome;
> Painted in Paris, fiddled in Leipsic,
> Summered at Homburg; and then, came home.

MISS Landon was eighteen when the snow-plough picked her up in the thorough-cut on the Pacific Slope and pitched her into the arms of Conductor McGuire. A year later, when her father retired, he was a rich man. At the suggestion of a widowed sister, the ex-merchant, his daughter, and the widow went abroad. At twenty-two she had been "finished" by travel, and heart-whole, was headed for home. She had seen a great deal of people and things. She had been wooed by an Italian count and had had a brush with a baron at Berlin, but she had never been thrilled as she had been with the touch of the hand and the sound of the voice of McGuire. She was probably the only American heiress who had given any attention to the poorly paid conductors of the European railways; the shabby guards, who run along the platform in soiled uniforms, cry the name of the station, flourish a flag, and open and shut the doors. Her conductor was as well dressed, as handsome, as intelligent, and almost as well paid as the captain of an Atlantic liner. These poor beggars were dirtier than the average second cabin deck-steward.

She was forever making comparisons, and wondering why she did it. A thousand times she had recalled his ardent glance when, as he told her in unmistakable language the story of his love, he had kindled the first fire in her girlish heart, and it had not gone out.

Of course, he could never be anything to her, and yet, try as she would, she could not forget. Without knowing why, she had conceived a deep interest in railways. She watched the men at work, marked the coming and going of trains in various countries, the inferior train service and accommodation on the continental railways of Europe.

Lately she had been studying the financial reports of the various railways on both sides of the Atlantic, and reading the stock quotations.

This was probably because her father had invested a vast amount of money in a new road in the West. She remembered that she had been eager to have him do this, and now felt a certain amount of responsibility, and so was quietly educating herself.

She often wondered whether the handsome conductor had heard of the new road in which she had half her fortune.

At times she went so far as to fancy herself, when left alone in this unfeeling world, seeking advice from the man who had carried her out of the snow-bank. And then she would ask herself how he could help her, this obscure conductor of a narrow-gauge railroad that wound among the hills and ravines of the Rocky Mountains.

Mr. Landon had left his business in the hands of his solicitors, in whom he had perfect faith, and had given himself over to rest for the past four years. Upon his arrival in London he learned that the new road, in which he had invested, had been roughly handled; not by stockjobbers, who are the dread of small investors, but by competing lines. They had made the mistake which is so often made, of sending out, as manager, a well-educated, perfectly respectable, handsomely attired, but utterly incompetent son of a bondholder, who didn't know a stop signal from a three-throw switch. The road had lost money from the start, but a rich and indulgent father had insisted upon keeping the young man as manager, and it was not until a well-known railway king had secured a controlling interest that the young man was permitted to return to his tandem and pink tea.

Things were going better, lately, he learned, since the road had been in the hands of a "native manager," and so the capitalist and his charming daughter spent another year in London.

"Papa," said Miss Landon, from her storm-blanket, one day in mid-ocean, "do you know a great deal of the success of this company is due to the employees?"

"Yes."

"Well, it's the same on a railway."

"Ah, Kate," laughed her father, "you're always railroading."

"Well, I was just thinking (she paused for just a breath) that if that young Mr. McGuire is still conductor (another impediment) you ought to try and get him on our road."

"Now, whatever made you think of that handsome young Irishman?"

"Well —"

"Well?—"

At that moment the band having assembled on deck, not twenty feet away, struck up a lively quickstep, and the sound of the E flat thrilled Miss Landon, as she had not been thrilled since she came out of her teens. She knew that tune, though she had heard it but once, and as the leading cornet walked up through the air, the words came to her:—

"Arrah, Patsy ! git up f'om th' fire,
    An' guv th' mon a sate;
Can't ye see that it's Misther McGuire,
    Come a courtin' yer sisther Kate?"

No man can make money or acquire fame without accumulating enemies; that's the price of success. To be sure they may not be all big men, sometimes not more than two by four, but they can make trouble. A Boston attorney, who looked after the interest and voted the stock of the absent shareholder in the Inter-mountain Air Line, had become the enemy of General Manager McGuire. This attorney had had the misfortune to pass through college with young Van Swell, who had made such a mess of managing the new road, and who had been forced to resign to make room for a real railroad man, so, to use a very expressive railroad expression, 'he had it in for" the new General Manager. He was a man of influence, and, when not otherwise engaged, he worked among the directors, many of whom he knew intimately, and his work was always against McGuire. The railway king, who had been the means of making McGuire General Manager, had been able to do so by influencing certain shareholders, and when the Boston attorney had won two or three of these to his side, the old faction could control the next election. They would not ask or expect the resignation of the brilliant young manager. So long as he was content with that position they could not, in their own interests, ask him to resign. But he was ambitious. Some of his friends had been putting his name forward as the next president, and that was wormwood and gall to the Van Swell contingent. These rumors, rife in clubs and hotel lobbies, soon reached the newspapers, and so the public. As the date for the meeting of the stockholders drew near, the matter became the leading topic in the daily press. The stock of the Intermountain Air Line became sensitive to the newspaper comments. Every man who had a dollar in the enterprise was uneasy. Men who lived like undertakers, off the misfortunes of others, who made money only when some one else lost, knew not whether to buy or sell. If the election could take place now, they could give a good guess that young Van Swell would be the next president. If a certain man who had been abroad for three or four years returned, took the advice of his friends and voted his stock instead of allowing his lawyer to vote it, things might be different. A bushel or more letters had been following this important, though somewhat indifferent, shareholder all over Europe. They had arrived in London only the day after the important individual had sailed for New York. Being a modest man, who considered his comings and goings of little importance to the general public, he had not taken the trouble to notify his friends of his intentions, but when a list of "distinguished" passengers had been cabled over, there was a little flurry in Wall Street. The friends of McGuire were enthusiastic. McGuire was indifferent. His friends wired him to come East and make a fight for the great prize that seemed almost within his grasp. He refused to budge. The bright young men who "did the railroads" on the daily papers had fun with Van Swell. They wondered whether he would take his valet and his yacht to the mountains with him. For a week and a day the excitement was at fever heat, but out in the Rockies, where the first frost was touching the oak and the aspen with silver and gold, the General Manager of the Air Line kept perfectly cool. The loyal employees, who had inklings of the doings of the pink-tea contingent at the East, spoke gently, almost reverently, to the General Manager. It would be a pity to lose him, people said, and many of the leading shippers said openly that they would give the Air Line no business if the town lost this genial official. The switchmen "offered" to strike. Of all the people interested, directly or indirectly, McGuire showed the least anxiety. Finally, the knowing ones guessed the cause of his indifference, which was now beginning to alarm his enemies. He had things "cut and dried," said the knowing ones, and it began to look that way. But it was not so. There was a shadow upon the heart of the General Manager. Few men in America had made greater success or reached a higher place in the railway world in a lifetime than this man had gained in thirty-five years, and yet he was not happy.

Now, as the time for the election of a new president drew near, the pressure became so great and the cry for McGuire at the seat of war grew so loud, that the General Manager yielded, reluctantly, and made ready for the journey. He might have carried his private car, for there was not a line between the Atlantic and the Pacific that would hesitate to handle it; but he contented himself with the section to which his Pullman pass entitled him, and his annual transportation. So quietly did he depart that none of the papers knew of it until he was far out on the plains. He had never been in Boston. She might be living there and now. As the train bore him out toward the Atlantic he began to wonder whether he might see her driving in the park with her dignified old father or (he dreaded the thought) with her husband.

CHAPTER XXI

ON A ROLLING SEA

WHEN the band ceased playing, Miss Landon's father had closed his eyes and had doubtless forgotten that his daughter had mentioned the conductor of the snow-bound train in which they had once travelled. But she had not forgotten, and now sat musing on the past and dreaming of the future. The sea was dead calm, and but for the vibration of the ship, caused by the machinery, and the slight lifting and lowering of the huge vessel as she ploughed through the ocean, one might have fancied that she was riding at anchor. The sun shone dimly through an autumn haze. Here and there the curving spine of a leaping porpoise split the surface of the silver sea, that lay like a great drop of molten lead. Far out toward the banks a whale was spouting like a hose at a fire. Now the big liner turns from her path to nose about an old scow that is drifting, bottom side up, with the current of the sea. A halfdozen gulls with steady wing stand above the stern of the ship. Some of the passengers are walking, some are dozing, others are reading, and all are apparently perfectly contented. As the sun went down the sea came up, and the big ship began to roll. When it was dark, save for the stars that stood above the ship, she began to pitch. One by one the women left their places and went below. When the bugle sounded for dinner not all the men and a very few women sat down in the great dining-hall. The neglected tables groaned under the good things that were left untouched. The band played cheerily in the little bower above, while the white-gloved stewards hurried out with the empties, and came back with the nuts and pudding and electric ice-cream. Before the meal was over the ship was rolling so that they had to lash on the sideboards. Only one woman remained at the captain's table. She was a good sailor. Presently the big ship lifted her nose until all the people held on to the tables, and then she gave a twist and came down on one corner. She went so low that the sea came up and wet all the windows. It reached up to the promenade deck, leaped to the bridge, over the ladies' saloon, and tore away six yards of the canvas fence, behind which the captain stands. It came along the deck, a solid stream, two feet and a half deep. It gathered up all the steamer chairs and drove them in a drift against the fence that marks the line between the first and second class. The people, men and women, who had stayed upon deck, were washed along, and piled up among the chairs. Mr. Landon, who was a poor sailor, slid out of his chair that was lashed to a railing that ran along the wall, and went, half bent, head first, for the heavy fence that runs round the ship. He ran so fast, when the ship sat on edge, that he could not straighten up, and before any one could reach him his head hit the railing. He went down like a man under a sandbag, and then the flood came and heaped the company's property and a lot of people on top of him. When the sea went down from the deck, and they gathered the old man up he was dead, — but he came to again.

A thoughtful and sympathetic woman rushed down to the dining-saloon and broke the news of the accident to the handsome young woman who was smiling over a glass of champagne at the captain.

"Oh! Miss Landon! yo' father's dead."

Miss Landon put down the glass and got to her feet. She swayed a bit, and the captain steadied her. "Is that true?" she asked, gazing at the woman.

"Well, he was; he's better now; he — "

"Thank you. It was thoughtful of you to come and tell me."

With the help of the captain and the chief steward (for the ship was rolling) she passed out. She was very pale, but there was just a hint of a smile upon her handsome face.

The sympathetic, thoughtful woman sank into a chair, and looked foolish.

When the ship's doctor had bathed the old gentleman's face and whipped over the rent in his scalp, he was able to talk to his daughter.

His sister, the girl's aunt, was helplessly sea-sick, and if there is a time in a man's life, or a woman's life, when a man or a woman is utterly incapable of sympathy for any human being who is foolish enough to want to live, it is when a man or woman is helplessly seasick.

"Papa was wholly unconscious for ten minutes, auntie," said Kate.

"Oh, how glorious! If I could only put this — umph! horrid — Oh! ship and this heaving, tossing sea, and every — umph! thing and everybody out of my mind, and then get out myself, for ten minutes, I'd strangle the doctor who brought me back to this miserable, howling, rolling, watery old world."

In spite of her troubles (she was not feeling any too fit herself) Miss Landon laughed at this pessimistic tirade from her usually even-tempered aunt.

CHAPTER XXII

THE NEW PRESIDENT

THAT night Miss Landon lay in her narrow bed, made short-stops of her elbows, and listened to the lash and roar of the rolling sea. At times the ship sank so deep into the main that one would fancy the keel scraping the bottom of the Atlantic. Nowhere in this world does one feel one's insignificance and utter helplessness more than at mid-ocean in such a sea. Miss Landon found herself thinking how helpless she would be in the world if that kind, indulgent father were to pass away. Half her fortune was invested in a railway along with the fortunes of friends and neighbors, who knew nothing about the business. Naturally enough her mind went back to her own experience on a mountain railroad, and to the handsome conductor. She went to sleep thinking of McGuire, dreamed of McGuire, and woke up with McGuire fresh in her mind, and marvelled at it.

For three days and nights the sea rushed past the rolling ship, and Landon lay in a semi-sane condition.

Finally, at dawn one day, the ship slowed down and picked up a pilot out of a small boat that was floundering in the ocean and apparently enjoying it.

"I want to see one of your passengers, a Mr. Landon, before I go upon the bridge, captain," said the man.

"Mr. Landon is not fit to be seen," said the captain. "He had an accident Monday afternoon off the banks."

"But I *must* see him, captain."

"Well, you persistent old salt, if you *must*, then take my advice and see his daughter, she's a whole lot better-looking."

"I have a very important message for your father, Miss Landon," said the pilot, making a sailor's bow.

"Thank you, I'll take it."

"But — I have sworn to give it into no hands but his, and I —"

"Can't trust me?"

"Oh, yes, miss — but —"

Now the poor man had become so confused that he had allowed the handsome, irresistible young woman to take the letter. She tore it open, glanced at the signature, and said, "Oh, this is all right, it's from papa's former business partner. He wants papa to do nothing until he sees him. Well, I'm sure he won't do much, poor dear."

"Then you'll be responsible, miss?"

"Oh, yes, I'll be responsible."

The pilot bowed again and ran up the ladder.

When the big ship crawled up through the fog, slowed again and picked up the Government trunk-riflers, a man throw up a lump of coal with a letter and a five-dollar note held to it by a rubber band.

"Keep the dough and give that letter to Landon," the man called up to the deck steward who had caught the coal.

When Miss Landon had opened this letter, which was from her father's solicitor, whom she disliked, she laughed. "'Do nothing until you see me.' I never saw such a lot of do-nothing people."

Now another tug came nosing up to the

liner, as a herring noses about a floating biscuit, and up came another lump of coal with a note and a dollar. The note was addressed to Mr. Landon, and stated that the "Daily Broker" would like to speak to him. Miss Landon crumpled the paper in her hand, leaned over the railing and looked down upon the paper man who had his chin pointed at the funnels of the big boat.

A man with a happy, round red face leaned over the side and said, "You can't see Mr. Landon."

"Why?"

"He's hurted."

"Bad?"

"Purty bad."

When the "Daily Broker's" extra edition came out with the elaborate account of the distressing accident to Mr. Landon, there was excitement in Wall Street. Naturally the Van Swells, while deeply deploring the accident to the estimable old Yankee, were elated at the prospect of his being unable to vote at the election which would take place in three days.

The "Daily Broker" told how the old man had gone, against the captain's protest, upon the hurricane deck when the ship was rolling, had slipped and fallen down the narrow ladder, broken his left arm and three ribs. These wounds, the paper said, were not necessarily fatal, but it was thought by the ship's doctor — who being slightly deaf talked very low, as deaf people do — that the venerable New Englander had sustained serious internal injuries.

Nearly every one had left the steamer when Miss Landon came down the gangway, followed by four stewards carrying her father, who, being rich, was attended by the ship's surgeon. Miss Landon was bewildered by the crowd of brokers, reporters, and friends assembled at the steamer. She had never dreamed that the Landons were of such importance. Her aunt took little note of anything, being obliged to pinch herself to see whether she still lived. The ship's surgeon, appreciating the importance of his patient, refused to allow even the most intimate friends of the injured man to speak to him. He went with them to their hotel and remained until another physician could be called. The new doctor was worse, if anything, than the ship's doctor. This was a severe blow to the solicitor, who knew better than to try to get to his client *via* the daughter.

On the following day Miss Landon persuaded the doctor to allow her father's old business partner and neighbor from Gloucester to see the sick man. Landon's mind was still wavy, but in the course of a half-hour's talk the visitor made it pretty clear to the injured man that if the Van Swells got control of the road, in which they were deeply interested, they would be likely to be squeezed out; if not, the road, under such incompetent management, would be sure to lose money.

"It's Kate's money," said the sufferer. "She railroads all the time, let her use her judgment," and it was so agreed.

The day before the date on which the election was to take place they moved on to Boston. When they were established in a comfortable hotel, their Gloucester friend asked to be allowed to introduce the gentleman who was being brought forward, without any effort upon his part, as the choice for President of the anti-Van Swell faction, to which the Landons rightfully belonged.

Now when the army of reporters saw the stranger going up in tow of the Gloucester man, they knew that the pink-tea people were beaten, for Landon's vote was sure to elect — it was the balance of power.

"This is Mr. McGuire, Miss Landon," said the Gloucester man.

McGuire, who was utterly indifferent to most people and most things in this world, was visibly affected. Miss Landon, who had fainted but once, clutched at the back of her chair. McGuire, finding his voice and feet, stepped forward, saying, in far-away, tremulous tones, like a man talking in his sleep, " I think I have had the pleasure of meeting Miss Landon."

The Gloucester man managed to rally from his surprise and introduced " Auntie," who until now had not seen the distinguished railroader.

" Is it possible?" Miss Landon heard herself say right to the man's face.

At this moment a street piano under their windows broke loose with the then raging popular air : —

> "Arrah, Patsy! git up f'om th' fire,
>   An' guv th' mon a sate;
> Can't ye see that it's Misther McGuire,
>   Come a courtin' yer sisther Kate?"

"Yes," said McGuire, taking her hand again, "it is possible."

Two hours later the Gloucester man was handing a carefully prepared "interview" to the reporters.

Mr. Thomas McGuire, the brilliant young manager, who was a personal friend of Mr. Landon's, would be the next President of the Inter-Mountain Air Line. This arrangement, while tacitly understood beforehand, had been definitely agreed to at a conference between Mr. Landon and his friend and former partner, who would represent the injured man at the meeting to-morrow.

CHAPTER XXIII

THE MAID OF ERIN

"YOU sent for me?" asked the General Manager of the Vandalia.

"Yes," said the President. "You remember Tom McGuire?"

"Is he the fellow that rode a mule into the White Mail one morning at West Silver Creek?"

"The same freckled Thomas."

"Well, I can't say that I remember him, for I have never seen him; but I have not had an opportunity to forget the story of his having saved a couple of trains for the company. Every time I go down the Line someone reminds me of his heroism. It got to that pass that when I heard the car hit the East Bridge I looked up. In would come this man's father, who is now roadmaster on the west end, and say, 'There's phare Tommy —' and if I happened to be alone the conductor would break the great news to me, until I am sick of the story."

"Well," said the President, "this Thomas is coming over the road to-day. He has just been re-elected President and General Manager of the Inter-Mountain Air Line. He is bringing a wife with him; the daughter of one of the directors, and I want to arrange a little surprise for him."

"That means a special train, I suppose?"

"No, that would not surprise him, for they are running him special over the Pennsylvania. Do you think we could make time with his car on the White Mail?"

"Well, we can try it. I'll wire Sedgwick to give us the best engines on the road. It will please him, I dare say, to ride down on the White Mail."

"Please him! why the Van will get all the business that originates on the Inter-Mountain for the next hundred years."

"Shall you meet him at the train?"

"Ah, yes. We're very good friends; he did his first work for me when I was general passenger agent."

An hour later the office boy handed a piece of white paper to the Trainmaster, upon which was written:

"Put President McGuire's car, 'Maid of Erin,' on the White Mail to-night.   G. M."

"Who gave you this, boy?"
"G. M."
"Himself?"
"That same."
"Well, you take this back and ask him if he means the Night Express."

Presently the boy came back, stopped in front of the Trainmaster's desk, and startled the office by reading aloud:

"Trainmaster, St. Louis, Vandalia, Terre Haute and Indianapolis Railroad, Indianapolis: —

"Put President McGuire's car, 'Maid of Erin' on the White Mail to-night.   G. M."

"Who told you to read that?" shouted the indignant Trainmaster.

"The G. M. told me to read it to you and see that you understood it."

There was a mischievous twinkle in the boy's eye, and gore in the eye of the T. M.

The operators, bending over their keys, glanced at each other, but there were no comments. There is very little talking in the office where the despatchers work.

"Here, boy," said the Trainmaster, handing a piece of clip to the messenger. "Take that to the yardmaster." This order read:

"Hook the 'Maid of Erin' on the White Mail to-night."

"Who gave you this message?" demanded the yardmaster.

The boy was ready to explode with fun

"The T. M."

"Well, you go back, sonny, and ask him if he's off his nut, see?" The boy reached for the paper, but the man held it back. "Go and ask Mr. Gilroy to explain this to you," said the yardmaster. "Ask him if he means the White Mail or the Night Express."

Presently the boy came back, and, hooking his white light on his arm as he had seen passenger conductors do, he stood in the centre of the yardmaster's office, and, having first arrested the attention of the switchmen, engineers, and firemen who were "railroading" there, read aloud:

"To the yardmaster, St. Louis, Vandalia, Terre Haute, and Indianapolis Railroad, Indianapolis: —

"Hook the 'Maid of Erin' on the White Mail to-night. T. M."

"Damn your skin, kid, who told you to read that?"

"The T. M. Told me to read it to you and see that you understood it, see?"

The engine had just been coupled to the White Mail, that had come in carrying green signals, when the special, running as second section of No. 1, whistled in. The President of the Vandalia boarded the "Maid of Erin," introduced the General Manager, and they were in turn introduced to Mrs. McGuire. By this time a yard engine had dashed up out of a siding, picked up the car, and set her gently on behind the White Mail.

"What time shall we reach the river?" asked the President of the Inter-Mountain.

"At 7.50," said the President of the Vandalia. "Possibly 7.49, but it will not be 51, Tommy, you can bet on that."

"To-morrow night," said McGuire, surprised but smiling. "How pokey you are!"

"To-morrow morning, if you please."

"What, you're not running us special? Now I don't want you to do that."

"No, you are going on a regular train," said the Van man.

"Then," said McGuire, waving his hand enthusiastically, "we're on the White Mail. Kate, do you hear? we're going through on the White Mail to-night. Say, this is —"

"Good-night! Good-bye," said the officials, for the car was going. The yard engine was giving them a kick out over the switches, and by the time the President and General Manager got to the rear platform the train was making fifteen miles an hour. The headlights of the pony shone full upon the happy faces of the bride and groom on the rear of the "Maid of Erin," and with a hurried last good-night, the two officials dropped off, one on either side.

They had long since ceased to carry passengers on the White Mail, and the engineer, who is not always consulted, wondered why they hung back so that night.

This "Maid of Erin" car had a false bottom, and between the two floors there was a layer of forty-five pound steel rails, laid close together, to weight her down and make her ride easy. At Terre Haute, the engineer called the conductor: "What in thunder you got on behind there to-night, Jack?"

"Private car — 'Maid of Erin.'"

"Huh!" said the old driver, "I thought, way the dam thing pulled, it must be made o' lead."

When the conductor learned at Terre Haute that the man in the private car was President McGuire, Thomas McGuire, freckled Tommy, who used to run the pump at West Silver Creek, he could scarcely wait until they pulled out before going in to see the great railroad man.

When they had passed over the last switch the conductor went back. McGuire turned and glanced at the man in the bright uniform.

"I beg pardon," stammered the conductor, "I thought you were alone."

"Oh, don't mention it, we're railroad people — sit down. I assure you that you could not be more welcome."

"But — I was looking for Mr. McGuire — I thought he might — well, we used to work together at Silver Creek."

"Is your name Connor?"

"Yes, sir."

"I thought so. Now have you been on this train since you left Indianapolis, and just now showed up?"

"But, you're not Tom — Mr. McGuire?"

"Yes, — I — am — Tom Mr. McGuire," and the President took the two hands of the sallow conductor and looked into his face.

"Katie," he said suddenly, "this is Jack Connor — little Jack that helped me detect the train robbers when we were hiding from the police. Shake hands with Mrs. McGuire, Jack, and then sit down."

Mrs. McGuire had been sleeping for two hours. Jack had, at McGuire's request, been telling him all his troubles. Things were going from bad to worse. The Engineers and Firemen were organized to fight, but the O. R. C., the conductors' organization, was opposed to strikes, and he, this restless, unhappy soul, was working hard and hopefully for the formation of a colossal union of all railroad organizations, against which the soulless corporations could not prevail.

"But what's the good of all this work and worry, Jack?"

"For mutual protection. For the general welfare of workingmen."

"Oh, workingmen be hanged! are n't we all workingmen? Wait till you are President of a railroad, Jack. When your nerves are shaken and your head roars when you go to bed, and you lie awake half the night trying to work out a scheme by which you can save a few millions to the soulless corporation that is clubbing the wolf away from your door, and, incidentally, save your reputation and your job, then you will know what it is to be a workingman."

Jack smiled pathetically, and glanced about at the rich hangings and expensive furnishings.

"I know what you are thinking now. You are saying, Tommy seems to be having a pretty good time. Well, did you ever see a drunk man who did n't *seem* to be having fun? I 'm just married."

President McGuire had intended to offer his old playmate a position on the Air Line, but when he had heard him discourse for a couple of hours on the relations of "Capital and Labor," he changed his mind. "A man who is always hugging a grievance will forget to flag," was what passed through the President's mind, and he concluded to leave his old friend on his native heath, where he was least liable to get into trouble.

"Jack, my boy," said McGuire, with his hand on the door of his stateroom, "you 're on the wrong leg of the 'Y,' and you 'll be throwing sixes all your life unless you switch. If I work hard and get to the front, and you work hard and get to the front — if each man takes care of his own job, always lending a helping hand to a fellow-worker when he can, there won't be many misfits or failures, Jack.— Good-night."

CHAPTER XXIV

OVER THE BIG BRIDGE

DENIS McGuire's successor in the little shanty down by the bridge had shown a white light to the driver of the Midnight Express, and was up, and out with the dawn, to show a milk-white flag to the men on the White Mail in the morning.

Down at East St. Louis, Roadmaster McGuire and Mrs. McGuire, who, in addition to being "the President's mother," continued to make herself generally useful about the house, were crossing the big bridge in order to be at the Union depot when the White Mail came in with the "Maid of Erin."

McGuire had been called early, and at dawn, when the black steed stopped to drink at Highland, Mrs. McGuire joined him. The President tried hard to appreciate the situation. Here was the realization of a dream that he had not dared dream in his happiest and most hopeful moods. He was going over the Silver Creek bridge on the White Mail and in his own private car, and he tried to feel perfectly satisfied with himself and the world. If he could only work himself up to feeling as proud and important as he did the day he took charge of the mule, the tank, and all the company's property at West Silver Creek, he would be glad, but it would not go. He was really a great man now, and that enabled him to appreciate what a little bit of a hole would be left if one great man were to be pulled out of the world.

The engine screamed. "That's St. Jacobs," said McGuire to his wife, and the station was behind them. Here the President had his first disappointment. The man who stood upon the platform in his shirt sleeves was a stranger. The old agent was in Texas. Now the train sank into the sag at East Silver, lifted again, as an ocean steamer lifts her huge form over a high sea, screamed on the ridge, and then went roaring down toward the bridge. How dwarfed and mean things looked! The old saw-mill was gone, and only a brown heap of sawdust marked the place. The mill-pond, into which he had taken many a run and jump from the railroad grade, was a slimy, stagnant pool covered with green scum.

"Now look, dear! — here — there! There's where the White Mail got mixed up with me and the mule."

"But where's the bridge, dear? Show me the bridge you used to guard, and the —"

"There, that's it. Is n't it little? Why, I used to fancy that was about the biggest bridge on the road."

"But you're a big boy now, Tommy," said his wife, patting him playfully on the back, "and things look different."

The whistle sounded again, and the "Maid of Erin" whipped round the curve at Hagler's tank.

There was a steady pull against the grade for a few moments, and then the President felt the train falling into the broad bottoms and saw the bluffs lift in their wake. He turned, and stole a look at the handsome woman who had left a luxurious home on the Atlantic to follow him into the West. He began now to appreciate his prize, and his other successes grew insignificant and mean, like the bridge, and the pond, and the mill-site. Feeling his glance, she turned her smiling face to him, bright and beautiful as the breaking morn, and he thought then that he had tasted what men call happiness.

With a rush and a roar, they swept up the incline, and McGuire, glancing up and down the river, said, as a man might say in a dream: "We're crossing the big bridge on the White Mail."

www.ingramcontent.com/pod-product-compliance
Lightning Source LLC
Chambersburg PA
CBHW020922230426
43666CB00008B/1534